DISCERNMENT

DISCERNMENT

Reading the Signs of Daily Life

HENRI J. M. NOUWEN

with Michael J. Christensen
and Rebecca J. Laird

HarperOne
An Imprint of HarperCollinsPublishers

HarperOne

DISCERNMENT: *Reading the Signs of Daily Life*. Copyright © 2013 by the estate of Henri J. M. Nouwen with Michael J. Christensen and Rebecca J. Laird. All rights reserved. Printed in the United States of America. No part of this book may be used or reproduced in any manner whatsoever without written permission except in the case of brief quotations embodied in critical articles and reviews. For information, address HarperCollins Publishers, 10 East 53rd Street, New York, NY 10022.

HarperCollins books may be purchased for educational, business, or sales promotional use. For information, please e-mail the Special Markets Department at SPsales@harpercollins.com.

HarperCollins website: http://www.harpercollins.com

HarperCollins®, ■®, and HarperOne™
are trademarks of HarperCollins Publishers.

FIRST EDITION

Library of Congress Cataloging-in-Publication Data
Nouwen, Henri J. M.
Discernment : reading the signs of daily life / Henri Nouwen, with
Michael J. Christensen and Rebecca J. Laird. — 1st ed.
pages cm
Includes bibliographical references.
ISBN 978-0-06-168615-3
1. Discernment (Christian theology) I. Title.
BV4509.5.N68 2013
248.4—dc23
2013004593

13 14 15 16 17 RRD(H) 10 9 8 7 6 5 4 3 2 1

Contents

Acknowledgments

This third volume completes the spiritual trilogy presenting Henri Nouwen's distinctive approach to contemplation, community, and compassion in the world through *spiritual direction, formation*, and *discernment*. All three volumes were developed from original materials found in the Henri J. M. Nouwen Archives in the Kelly Library, Saint Michael's College, University of Toronto, with the support and cooperation of the Henri J. M. Nouwen Estate and Nouwen Legacy Trust.

We especially want to thank Kathy Smith and Maureen Wright with the Nouwen Legacy Trust, and Jessica Barr, assistant archivist at the Nouwen Archives, for their generous time and support in locating materials for us in the library. We also gratefully acknowledge the publishing team at HarperOne, especially our relentless editor, Roger Freet, without whose persistence this final volume would not have been completed. Also, we thank our excellent production editor, Alison Petersen, publicist Julie Baker, and Janelle Agius in marketing.

Sue Mosteller, literary executrix, who took an active role in the previous two volumes, worked especially hard on this final volume, which we all agree was the hardest to compile and develop from the Nouwen journals and available resources. For

Sue's multiple reviews, constructive critiques, compassionate style, and generous support, we are deeply grateful.

John Mogabgab, Henri's teaching assistant at Yale and current editor of *Weavings,* gave us the lead that started us on developing this work. John, Henri's editor for "The Genesee Diary," revealed that only about one-third of what Henri wrote in his diary was eventually published and suggested that the original three volumes of "The Genesee Diary" would be a good place to start in looking for his spiritual discernment process and unpublished reflections. This proved right and led to many such unpublished reflections on discernment in other Nouwen journals. Thank you, John, for the lead and your encouragement in this three-year process.

We appreciate Robert A. Jonas for agreeing to write the foreword (and an appendix) to this volume. A former Harvard student and close friend of Henri Nouwen's, and now our good friend and colleague, Jonas (as he likes to be called) helped us process the structure and approach to this book. He offers his own unique vision of discernment by employing the marvelous metaphor of *sailing the seas* true north determined by the wind, sea, and sails, as well as the company on board the ship. We hope the reflection he prepared for this work will find its way into his own writing on spiritual practice.

Finally, we want to thank our youngest daughter, Megan, for typing many excerpts into a text that was finally woven into this book. Now in college, Megan, at three and a half years of age, once sat on Henri's lap at our home, two months before he died in 1996, and asked him an important question: "How big is God?" Henri responded with a mystic's insight: "God is as big as your heart; and your heart is as big and wide as the universe." A good answer, repeated often in our household.

And so to the memory of Henri Nouwen and the image of him holding a little child on his lap and leading us to the unfathomable love of God, we dedicate this labor of love entitled simply *Discernment.*

PREFACE
What This Book Is About

The premise of this book is that God is always speaking to us—individually and as the people of God—at different times and in many ways: through dreams and visions, prophets and messengers, scripture and tradition, experience and reason, nature and events. And that *discernment* is the spiritual practice that accesses and seeks to understand what God is trying to say.

When we are rooted in prayer and solitude and form part of a community of faith, certain signs are given to us in daily life as we struggle for answers to spiritual questions. The books we read, the nature we enjoy, the people we meet, and the events we experience contain within themselves signs of God's presence and guidance day by day. When certain poems or scripture verses speak to us in a special way, when nature sings and creation reveals its glory, when particular people seem to be placed in our path, when a critical or current event seems full of meaning, it's time to pay attention to the divine purposes to which they point. Discernment is a way to read the signs and recognize divine messages. Henri Nouwen is a trustworthy guide in this ancient spiritual practice.

Discernment: Reading the Signs of Daily Life, the third and final volume of Nouwen's posthumous spiritual trilogy, builds on the previous volumes as it moves the reader from *questions* to *movements* to *signs.* The first volume, *Spiritual Direction* (HarperOne, 2006), is about *living the questions of the spiritual life* (Who am I? What am I called to do? Who is God for me?). The second volume, *Spiritual Formation* (HarperOne, 2010), is about *following the movements of the Spirit* (from resentment to gratitude, fear to love, denying to befriending death). This third volume, *Discernment,* is about *reading the signs of daily life* (primarily seen in books, nature, people, and events).

Discernment follows Nouwen's journals and other writings, focusing on what he has to say about discernment and vocation for today. Characteristically informed by biblical insights and patterns of the church year, the book is divided into three parts: 1) the nature of discernment, including the spiritual gift and scriptural practice of distinguishing spirits of truth from falsehood; 2) the process of seeking God's guidance in books, nature, people, and events; and 3) ways of discerning vocation, presence, identity, and time for divine purpose.

For Henri Nouwen, *spiritual discernment* is hearing a deeper sound beneath the noise of ordinary life and seeing through appearances to the *interconnectedness* of all things, to gain a vision of how things hang together (*theoria physike*) in our lives and in the world. Biblically, *discernment* is spiritual understanding and experiential knowledge, acquired through disciplined spiritual practice, of how God is active in our lives, which leads to a life "worthy of our calling" (Col. 1:9). It is a spiritual gift and practice that "ascertains and affirms the unique way God's love and direction are manifested in our lives, so that we can know God's will and fulfill our calling and mission within the mysterious inter-workings of God's love."[1]

But, as all who attempt to live the questions and follow the movements of the Spirit know, discernment is not a step-by-step program or a systematic pattern. Rather, it is a regular discipline of listening to the still, small voice beneath the rush of the whirlwind, a prayerful practice of reading the subtle signs in daily life. Discernment is not once-and-for-all decision making at critical points in one's life (Should I take this job? Whom should I marry? Where should I live and work?), but a lifelong commitment to "remember God" (*memoria Dei*), know who you are, and pay close attention to what the Spirit is saying today.

Because Nouwen situates discernment in both a personal and a community context, we have organized his approach in three parts according to common themes of the journey of faith. Rather than offering a systematic presentation of the process, the themes presented are condensed and adapted from the whole of Nouwen's corpus, published and unpublished, culled mostly from his journals and previously unpublished reflections but supplemented by excerpts from published writings.

In part 1, Nouwen defines the gift and practice of discernment as rooted in the core disciplines of the Christian life: prayer, community, worship, and ministry. He shares his firsthand experience of what he calls "fighting the demon" as part of the ancient biblical practice of "discernment of spirits." He invites his readers—and shows us how—to embrace the struggle and trust in the power of God, to resist the spirit of darkness and live in the light of God, who reminds us that we are beloved.

Part 2 describes what Nouwen learned from his mentor, Thomas Merton, and from his own experience of reading the signs of God's presence and finding daily guidance in the Bible and other books, nature's beauty, people in our path, and current and critical events in our life.

Part 3 engages what might be called Nouwen's "spirituality of discernment." Readers familiar with his major themes in other works will recognize vintage Nouwen here and will gain new insights about our core identity as God's beloved children; experiencing the divine presence in the human heart (*memoria Dei*) through discernment; and knowing *when to act, when to wait,* and *when to be led* or acted upon, according to *God's time* (*kairos*), which is the purpose of discernment.

HOW THIS VOLUME WAS WRITTEN

While the first two volumes of this trilogy were developed primarily from lecture notes and reflections for the courses he taught at Yale Divinity School and Harvard Divinity School in the 1980s, the present volume draws primarily from unpublished portions of his discernment journals over twenty-five years: "On Retreat: Genesee Diary" (1974) published as *The Genesee Diary;* "South American Diary" (1981-1982) published as *Gracias!;* "The L'Arche Journal" (1985-1986) published as *The Road to Daybreak,* "Ukrainian Diary" (1996) unpublished; and "Sabbatical Journal" (1996) published as *Sabbatical Journey.* We attempted to compile in one volume most of what Nouwen had to say about discernment, weaving the fragments together with lessons he learned from classical Christian writers like Teresa of Avila and Jean-Pierre de Caussade, contemporary mentors like Thomas Merton and Jean Vanier, and his favorite mystics and saints. Such a redaction required the support and cooperation of the Nouwen Literary Trust, without which the book would be only a compilation of quoted material.

How This Book Can Be Read

Most of Nouwen's books are short enough to be read either in a day or two or slowly over a few weeks of devotional practice. We recommend reading this book in three part segments, over a period of several weeks, perhaps during the season of Advent or Lent.

One good way to begin is to simply choose which part to read first. While there's no need to read the major parts in order, within each part, it is best to read the chapters sequentially.

If you belong to a book study or spiritual practice group, try reading a chapter each week for ten weeks. Or use the book in relation to a season of the church year. At the end of each chapter are exercises for deeper discernment that can be used for individual journaling or small-group sharing.

Those reading this book as part of an academic course or certification process in spiritual direction or formation may find the material in the appendix helpful for understanding Nouwen's distinctive approach to discernment. Robert Jonas's foreword, "Henri's Way of Discernment," and his appendix, "Spiritual Friendship and Mutual Discernment," provide good material for going deeper into the topic. Michael's appendix, "Henri Nouwen on Hearing a Deeper Beat," extends his use of Henry David Thoreau's metaphor of discernment as one who "hears the beat of a different drummer" and "steps to the music which he hears, however measured or far away" (*Walden*, ch 8)."

Finally, like the previous volumes, this book is best read devotionally and accompanied by regular spiritual practice. Nouwen provides detailed instructions on how to do *lectio divina* (spiritual reading) and *visio divina* (spiritual gazing) in contemplative prayer and meditation. If you have access to an audiotape by Nouwen, you may want to try *audio divina* (spiritual listening) in conjunction with your reading. For example, chapter 10, "Know the Time: When to Act, When to Wait, When to Be Led" would be enhanced by listening to Nouwen's audiotape *A Spirituality of Waiting* (Crossroads, 1995).

By living the questions, following the movements of the Spirit, and reading the signs of daily life, we can better live a spiritual life in a world with too many easy answers, conflicting movements, and confusing signs.

Michael J. Christensen and Rebecca J. Laird
Feast of the Epiphany 2013

Henri's Way of Discernment

by Robert A. Jonas

Henri was a very unusual Roman Catholic priest. He felt comfortable with Protestant ministers, Latin American peasants, urban intellectuals, U.S. senators, wealthy patrons, and the mentally and physically disabled. His books are cherished by millions of readers around the world, including celebrities like Fred Rogers and Bill Moyers and political leaders such as Hillary Rodham Clinton, who has stated publicly that Henri's book, *The Return of the Prodigal Son*, had a profound effect on her at a critical time.[1] Henri's parish was everywhere, and his congregation was everyone. He was a priest for all sorts of people and for all seasons of the human condition.

Over his nearly forty years of ordained life, Henri presided at the Eucharist almost every day and brought a sacred presence to hundreds of births, weddings, and funerals across North America, South America, and Europe. As a much sought-after counselor, mentor, and guide, he participated in countless individual pastoral conversations. He did not know how to type or to send email, but just about every day he wrote personal letters in a beautiful calligraphic script. Henri's followers savored the way that Henri deftly, reverently told the story of Jesus in a way that expressed his conviction that "Jesus's story is our story," and that we, like Jesus, are God's beloved.

Henri's life did not follow a familiar trajectory or keep to a predictable path. His journey makes perfect sense only when one looks back over its course. If one plays it forward, he was breaking new ground with just about every choice he made. For Henri, discernment was a daily practice. In fact, it was a moment-to-moment practice, because he found no model, no pattern for what he felt called to do. He stepped into the unknown like a tightrope walker stepping into nearly thin air, or like someone leaping from rock to rock across a stream in an impenetrable cloud. Somehow Jesus, his rock, would always rise up to meet his foot.

Henri learned from spiritual leaders that included Dom John Eudes Bamberger, the abbot of the Abbey of the Genesee, and Jean Vanier, the founder of L'Arche, and he had many friends, but in the end he trusted no one but Jesus to show him the way to God. For Henri, Jesus was the archetype of a fully discerning person, sensitive and responsive to God's presence in everything he did.

Henri was a genius in the art of spiritual spelunking as he explored the cave of the heart. Wearing the headlamp of the Holy Spirit, he reached out for every available tool to break new ground—theological wisdom, psychological insights, scripture, the writings of Christian mystics and saints, teachings from other religious traditions, literature, the arts, prayer, academic research, and world travel. Henri believed that he had discovered the living waters of spiritual awakening in Jesus Christ, and he dedicated his whole life to the process of inviting others to drink from those eternal streams. For Henri, Jesus was the light that shone in the darkness—the gateway, the healer, the deliverer, the inspiration and guide for anyone who seeks to live from the infinite place in the heart from which Jesus lived.

Henri emphasized that Christian discernment is not the same as decision making. Reaching a decision can be straightforward: we consider our goals and options; maybe we list the pros and cons of each possible choice; and then we choose the action that meets our goal most effectively. Discernment, on the other hand, is about listening and responding to that place within us where our deepest desires align with God's desire. As discerning people, we sift through our impulses, motives, and options to discover which ones lead us closer to divine love and compassion for ourselves and other people and which ones lead us further away.

In Henri's sermons and retreats, as well as in his thirty-five books, he highlighted a distinctive vision of Jesus Christ that was thoroughly grounded in scripture and Catholic theology. To understand what Henri meant by *discernment,* it's important to repeat that for Henri the name Jesus meant the eternal presence of the one who is God's continuing incarnation in human form. Henri was interested in the timeless dimension of Jesus Christ, the life that the crucified and risen Jesus shares with us now. According to Henri, the historical life of Jesus opened a new frontier in human experience so that the incarnation of Christ—which has no beginning and no end—could become an ongoing event for all human beings and, indeed, for all creation. Eventually, we can learn to discern the face of Christ everywhere and at all times. Henri's view often reminded me of the medieval Dominican friar, Meister Eckhart, who advised, "Expect God evenly in all things."

Henri understood the name of Jesus as the reality of the resurrected Christ who unites humanity and divinity. Jesus is the life of the divine that longs to become present in every moment of our ordinary existence. Henri trusted that a relationship with the timeless Jesus would gradually transform our lives, enacting a complete rapprochement between our will and God's will. Perhaps this alignment would be complete only after our deaths, but it would be complete. For Henri, the Christian liturgical language of time that is used for Christ—the one who was, is, and will be—describes the fullness of Jesus's presence. For those who have faith, Jesus was, is, and will be the divine archetype that animates our lives.

In Henri's view, discernment should proceed from a person's grounded, ordinary life. He did not want people to think that our goal is to escape from our everyday stresses and conflicts. Instead, we should invite the Holy Spirit into our direct experience, into our thoughts, memories, worries, and plans. Instead of seeking a life free from pain and suffering, we should trust that Jesus is present in our pain and suffering. We need to acknowledge our suffering honestly—our loneliness, regrets, sadness, hopelessness, and anger—and then open our hearts to the one who loves us in every detail of our lives. In this way, as Henri often said, our sorrow can turn to joy, our hostility to hospitality, and our loneliness to a solitude pregnant with possibilities. If we experience grief at the loss of a loved one, we should not simply tough it out or forcibly turn our attention to more pleasant things; rather we should let Jesus bear the loss with us. After all, as Henri would say, Jesus lost your loved one, too.

For Henri, the journey of discernment begins as soon as a person begins to seek God, the mystery who is the source of all that is. What tradition will help me find my way to my true self, my true vocation, and my true community? Where does my complete flowering as a human being connect with the needs of the world? Henri never said that Christianity is the only way or even the best path. It was *his* way; his own true north. He deeply believed that through faith in Jesus and with the help of a guide and a loving community of faith, each of us can become deeply rooted in a life that manifests the qualities we see in the life of the historical Jesus. For Henri, these qualities include those named as the fruit of the Spirit (Gal. 5:22–23): love, joy, peace, patience, kindness, generosity, faithfulness, gentleness, and self-control. Henri himself longed to embody these qualities, and his ministry was ardently focused on the question, How can I spread the word about the transforming path of Jesus, and how can I create contexts where people can hear the gospel message of love in fresh ways?

L'Arche communities are rooted in the Roman Catholic tradition, and during the ten years that he spent as pastor of the L'Arche Daybreak community in Toronto, Henri presided at the daily masses and at frequent baptisms, marriages, and funerals. He enjoyed introducing potential converts to the Roman Catholic Church, but he also worked with the rest of the staff to honor the non-Catholic faith traditions of core members of the community. Being a faithful Roman Catholic was his way, but he was at peace with the likelihood that it would never become everyone's way.

Henri supported hundreds of people around the world, serving as a friend, priest, and spiritual counselor. He was heartbroken when he saw people suffering because they were unaware of the gift of Christ's love. He was eager to help everyone—including himself—to remember who we really are: the beloved and chosen of God. Henri often declared, "If I am chosen, that doesn't mean that others are not chosen. When I really receive this gift of being God's beloved, I look around and see that all others are beloved, too!"

In one of his most popular books, *The Return of the Prodigal Son,* Henri reflects on the prodigal son who squandered his life but is nevertheless welcomed home to the unconditional embrace of a father whose loving hands represent the dual father-mother nature of God. If we experience this ultimate embrace as our own and if we receive this truth into our hearts—moment by moment, discernment comes more easily. It comes more easily because in receiving our belovedness, we receive the Holy Spirit into our hearts as the center of our knowing, feeling, and deciding. The Holy Spirit guides us without ever displacing our own empowered center of decision and discernment.

Henri understood that it is impossible to become spiritually mature all at once. He believed that we have inherited a tendency to forget our true identity as creatures of a caring, merciful God. Our true identity is that we are created in the image and likeness of our Creator, and that we are each the chosen and the beloved of God, just as Jesus was chosen and beloved. But then we forget—we sin, we are wayward, and especially when we feel afraid, we are self-centered. We resist knowing who we really are in God.

Henri believed that we can discern the depths of our lives and vocation only if we surrender our ego-centered view of reality. As everyone knows, this is hard to do. It is unsettling, even scary, to relinquish who we think we are, and scary to stop clinging to what we have and what we do. It is scary to step into the hidden, unknown dimension of our lives where we meet God. Of course, we may choose to follow a spiritual path that focuses on perfect conformity to the outward rules of a particular church or denomination, but allegiance to dogma and doctrine, to religious rules and outward behavior, can take us only so far. Only when we inwardly surrender our smaller, culturally formed identities can we open up to the Spirit who waits for us and longs to infuse our knowing and discerning with God's love. Through the narrow gate of this ego abdication, we find our truth, our true selves, and our vocation.

In this soul work of accepting our larger self in God, Henri faithfully followed Jesus's assertion that "those who find their life will lose it, and those who lose their life for my sake will find it" (Matt. 10:39 NRSV). Surrender sounds as if one is losing something, but in this case giving up leads paradoxically to freedom and to the discovery of our true selves. This is because the deep center of our selves is the Holy Spirit. Henri often pointed out that Jesus had vivid experiences of the Holy Spirit, that the Spirit was with Jesus at his baptism, and that the Spirit guided Jesus into deep solitude with God and into a victorious confrontation with evil (see Mark 1:12 and Luke 4:1). When we enter the story of Jesus, we see the Holy Spirit at work in him, and when we enter deeply into our own stories, we discover the Holy Spirit at work in our own lives, too. Remember, says Jesus, that "the Spirit of your Father [is] speaking through you" (Matt. 10:20 NRSV).

Henri believed that the Holy Spirit is an inner presence who is the deep center of our new life in Christ, a center from which discernment blossoms. Over time discernment becomes easier as we come to trust the knowing of the Spirit within us, but it always takes discipline to keep our focus. Like a sailor on the high seas, we need to remember our goal and intention, to put our trust in God, and to meditate on the qualities of Spirit that we want to embody. And we need to keep scanning our inner and outer lives to be sure that we are taking everything into account, scanning for signs of the Spirit's presence, noticing its invitations, and listening for what Henri called "the voice of the beloved."

Discernment is a discipline and practice that requires us to cultivate trust, love, faith, hope, and courage. We cannot see with perfect clarity what lies ahead. And we cannot see the Holy Spirit within us. In fact, we have no tangible evidence that the Holy Spirit has made a home in us. Accepting and daring to put our trust in this possibility is a matter of faith. We cannot control the Spirit: "The wind blows where it chooses, and you hear the sound of it, but you do not know where it comes from or where it goes. So it is with everyone who is born of the Spirit" (John 3:8 NRSV). To be born of the Spirit is to step into a freedom that we never imagined before. It is to trust that the Spirit knows us better than we know ourselves, and that we can therefore relinquish our smaller identities to become someone who is beyond our own understanding. We now accept that the mystery of God, which once seemed outside and beyond us, has made a home within us.

When we accept our complete belovedness, we stop judging ourselves and other people; as a result, other people begin to feel safe with us. When we open the hospitality of our hearts to the Spirit, the Spirit frees us to extend hospitality to our fellow humans and all God's creation. The Spirit's hospitality becomes ours, and we experience the alignment of our will with God's will—a traditional definition of successful discernment. What we want is what God wants. Paradoxically, we feel more truly ourselves than we have ever felt before.

Where does Henri Nouwen's path of discernment take us? Gradually we notice that our lives are becoming less chaotic and less filled with drama. We notice that we are less anxious and fearful. Although sometimes we may still feel knotted up with fear or anxiety, we notice that we are nevertheless able to step forward into the unknown to create something new, to offer help or to ask for help. We notice that we feel more comfortable with solitude and with accepting mystery and uncertainty, paradox and ambiguity. We find ourselves having more patience as we listen to those who are struggling. We discover that the deep inner peace we sometimes feel in solitude is also present when we are with others. We find that we are caught up in fewer inner dialogues in which we judge or blame ourselves or other people. These are all signs of the Spirit's presence.

The Spirit within us is free of ego-driven entanglements and confusions. The Holy Spirit is eternal and unchanging, yet she empties herself lovingly into our lives, taking up the form and dynamism of our particular lives and enlightening every aspect of our experience: our consciousness, as well as the quality and depth of our feeling, thinking, imagining, and listening. The Spirit within us brings us into a deep interconnectedness with others in love. Thus our bodies and lives participate in the body of Christ, and the Spirit is the dynamic, elastic presence that continually knits us into one.

Henri Nouwen believed that we can trust our inner experience as we grow up to our full stature in Christ. Like sailors on the sea of life, if we keep our eyes on the far horizon where Jesus beckons to us, we can trust that he will guide us true north. If we keep our hands on the wheel of the sailboat and allow the Spirit to fill our sails and guide us, we will find blessings even in our sorrows, even in our anger and loneliness. Our deepest identity is that place where the Holy Spirit lives, knows, loves, and guides from within our own awareness. It is the tacit horizon of all our knowing and discerning. Henri concludes one of his sermons (at the Crystal Cathedral in Garden Grove, California) with a declaration that lays the foundation for every question of discernment:

God has created you and me with a heart that only God's love can satisfy. And every other love will be partial, will be real, but limited, will be painful. And if we are willing to let the pain prune us, to give us a deeper sense of our belovedness, then we can be as free as Jesus and walk on this world and proclaim God's first love, wherever we go.[2]

INTRODUCTION
When There Is Darkness, Light
by Henri Nouwen

During the past few years I have experienced an increasing desire to write to all of you who have become part of that worldwide net in which I have been caught: close friends, past and current students, parishioners, correspondents, family, and community members. Today, more than ever, I think of all of you as a community. I belong to you and you to me, and we to each other, whether we know each other or not, whether we have met or not, whether we have embraced or not. We have been brought together by the goodness of God for reasons beyond our choosing and for the purposes of God.

I am staying in a small village, Saint Martin d'Aout, south of Lyon, France, to rest and pray. This tiny town perched on one of the low hills of the Drôme is pure paradise. It offers a breathtaking view of the undulating farmlands with their endless variation of yellows, greens, and blues, constantly changing in tone as the sun moves toward the mountain range on the far side of the Rhône. As I look at the wide, rolling fields of sunflowers and wheat, I have an inkling of what Vincent van Gogh felt when he let his eyes wander over the wheat fields of Arles.

As I sit in this quiet French church in front of the altar, surrounded by silent saints of ages past, I know that the time has come to gather you all together in my heart and speak to you in a way I could not before. A new vision is emerging in me that I want to talk to you about—a vision of who you are, and who I am, and who we are together. So I call you around me in this empty church: from Holland, Belgium, and France; from Bolivia, Peru, Nicaragua, and Mexico; from the United States and Canada; and from many other times and places. You are students, teachers, priests and ministers, lawyers, doctors, bankers, and engineers. You are rich and poor, busy and unemployed, and retired. You are happy and sad.

I do not think of myself as your teacher. I think of myself as a friend who has made a very long journey and has learned something so important that he does not want to keep it for himself. I have come to a place in my life where these obvious and beautiful differences among us seem small in the context of the unity that binds us all together. The unity of life among us is even deeper and stronger than the diversity between us.

Most of you, dear friends, I have come to know because of your questions, your pain, your worries, and your intense yearning for a deep understanding of the meaning of your lives. You have shown me your loneliness, your feelings of separation and alienation, your sense of not belonging, your emotional restlessness, your sexual frustration, your mental confusion, your anger at your parents, your teachers, your church, your society. You have shared with me the many ways you have attempted to find

peace in your minds and hearts. You met with counselors, psy-
chotherapists, and spiritual guides. You were part of all sorts of
healing sessions, workshops, and retreats. You often made radical
changes in lifestyle, courses of study, and profession.

Some of you rejected your past, and some of you accepted
age-old long-forgotten traditions. Some of you traveled to the
Far East and found there wise men and women to whom you
gave your trust. Some of you have come to the conclusion that
all religion is an illusion. Some of you have thrown off long-held
restrictions on self-expression and chosen to give free rein to the
deepest urges of your body and mind. Some of you have turned
away from the celebrated pleasures of the world and imposed
severe limits on the expression of your physical and emotional
needs. Some of you still have great ambitions about success and
popularity. Some of you are no longer looking for human praise
and have settled for a more hidden existence of Spirit.

All the directions you have chosen, all the choices you have
made—I know them in my own heart. There are few paths not
familiar to me. If you felt oppressed, I did, too. If you consulted
directors, I did the same. Like you, I have been excited about new
books and new theories, have put my hope in a new psychological
or spiritual movement, trusted a new hero, and given my energy
to a new way of changing myself or others. You and I are not very
different. We belong to a time and a society in which there are
few boundaries or forbidden paths.

Within the churches there are as many opinions and visions
as outside the churches. There is no virtue that is not called sin
somewhere, and no particular sin that is not called virtue somewhere else. Within a mile of each other, people say and think
diametrically opposed things, live diametrically opposed lives,
and act in diametrically opposed ways. There is an enormous
freedom to choose your own way of thinking, talking, or acting,
and whatever your choice, someone will praise you and someone
will blame you, but most likely very few will intervene. You and

I are on our own in a world of our own making. A frightening freedom. Who can live it and not get lost?

It seems that together you, my extended community, represent all the possible directions human beings can take. I see among you married and divorced friends, gay friends who live in a committed relationship and those who don't want to be restricted to one partner, celibate friends who are deeply committed to their single-minded and devoted lives, and those who experience their celibacy as oppressive and burdensome. I see among you friends who experience deep inner darkness and hardly know how to make it from day to day, and others so radiant with happiness that the future seems full of wonderful promises. I see friends with big money, big jobs, and big responsibilities, but I also see friends who can hardly survive, who wonder what to do with their time and have very little of which to be proud.

Whoever or wherever you are in your life, as I see you in front of me in prayer, I feel very close to you, not in any sentimental way, but as a man who has lived your lives interiorly and knows about the pain and joy you hold in your hearts. As I let my eyes look deeply into my own heart and yours, I am increasingly aware of how lost we are. Those of us who are wealthy and successful are no less lost than those of us who are poor and experience life as a failure. Those of us who are healthy and strong are no less lost than those of us who are frail and weak. Those of us who are priests and ministers are no less lost than those of us who are lawyers, doctors, or business people. Those of us who are active in the church and society are no less lost than those of us who have resigned ourselves to passive waiting for the end of life. Those of us who are excited about new projects or full of energy to bring about changes here and there are no less lost than those who have become skeptical or cynical about the possibility of a better world.

Apart from the love of God in our lives, we are people lost at sea, without anchors. We stand alone without supporting walls, without a floor to walk on, without a ceiling to protect us, without a hand to guide us, without eyes that look at us with love, without a companion to show the way.

Dear friends, we have to know the darkness to be able to search for the light. We first must come to know our lostness if we want to find meaning, purpose, and direction in life. What I want to share with you is a way out of the darkness, a way to find the light.

The way of discernment begins with prayer. Praying means breaking through the veil of existence and allowing yourself to be led by the vision that has become real to you, whatever you call that vision—"the Unseen Reality," "the Numen," "the Higher Power," "the Spirit," or "the Christ." Our prayers are directed not to ourselves but to Another, who wants to turn us around, who longs to be present, and who is able to guide us. The one who prays to God pierces the darkness and senses the source of all being.

This is a book about spiritual discernment. It begins with the context for discernment in solitude and community, and the practice of what the Bible calls "distinguishing spirits" of truth and falsehood. By embracing the darkness, in solitude and community, we eventually find the light. Divine guidance can be found in the books we read, the nature we enjoy, the people we meet, and the events we experience. Through the practice of discernment, we can test our calling and find vocation. We can open our hearts to the divine presence. We can discover who we really are. And we can ascertain when to act, when to wait, and when to be led. Spiritual discernment is an ancient Christian practice with many wells of wisdom from which to drink. These are the themes and chapters I want to share with you in the following pages. I hope and pray that you will take time to listen.

Your friend in life and death,
Henri [1]

PART ONE

What Is Discernment?

ONE

Embracing the Practice in Solitude and Community

We ask that you may be filled with the knowledge of God's will in all spiritual wisdom and understanding so that you may lead lives worthy of the Lord.

—*Colossians* 1:9–10 NRSV

Discernment is a spiritual understanding and an experiential knowledge of how God is active in daily life that is acquired through disciplined spiritual practice. Discernment is faithful living and listening to God's love and direction so that we can fulfill our individual calling and shared mission.

Definitions are a good place to begin, but let me sketch out some of the core affirmations and practices necessary to discernment. When I was living in a Trappist monastery as a temporary monk,[1] seeking to discern whether I was called to live the contemplative life or a more active life of teaching and ministry, I remember walking through a building where I hadn't been before. I came across a reproduction of Hazard Durfee's beautiful painting *The Flute Player* framed with an old but familiar text by Henry David Thoreau:

> Why should we be in such desperate haste to succeed, and in such desperate enterprises? If a man does not keep pace with his companions, perhaps it is because he hears a different drummer. Let him step to the music which he hears, however measured or far away.[2]

As I studied the quiet, concentrated face of Durfee's musician, I realized that discernment is like hearing a different drummer. I remembered that one of the books about Thomas Merton is called *A Different Drummer*.[3] Merton stepped away from the active, academic life and chose a contemplative life. I wondered if I was called to make that kind of move myself.

When I reflected on *The Flute Player*, I knew myself as restless and searching. I felt I was stumbling over my own compulsions and illusions way too often. During my time at Genesee, I began to understand that when we listen to the Spirit, we hear a deeper sound, a different beat. The great movement of the spiritual life is from a deaf, nonhearing life to a life of listening. From a life in which we experience ourselves as separated, isolated, and lonely to a life in which we hear the guiding and healing voice of God, who is with us and will never leave us alone. The many activities in which we are involved, the many concerns that occupy our time, the many sounds that surround us make it hard for us to hear the "still, small voice" through which God's presence and will are made known (1 Kings 19:12).

Living a spiritually mature life requires listening to God's voice within and among us. The great news of God's revelation is not simply that "I am," but also that God is actively present in the moments of our lives at all times and places. Our God is a God who cares, heals, guides, directs, challenges, confronts, corrects. To discern means first of all to listen to God, to pay attention to God's active presence, and to obey God's prompting, direction, leadings, and guidance.

I stepped away from my teaching to slow down for a time in intentional community. It was hard for me to see God at work in my life when I was running from class to class and traveling from place to place. I had so many classes to prepare, lectures to give, articles to finish, people to meet that I had come quite close to believing myself indispensable. Still I was frightened of being alone and having an unscheduled day, even as I longed for solitude and rest. I was full of paradoxes.

When we are spiritually deaf, we are not aware that anything important is happening in our lives. We keep running away from the present moment, and we try to create experiences that make our lives worthwhile. So we fill up our time to avoid the emptiness we otherwise would feel. When we are truly listening, we come to know that God is speaking to us, pointing the way, showing the direction. We simply need to learn to keep our ears open. Discernment is a life of listening to a deeper sound and marching to a different beat, a life in which we become "all ears."

What Does the Bible Say About Discernment?

Discernment is expressed concisely by the apostle Paul in the Letter to the Colossians: "We ask that you may be filled with the knowledge of God's will in all spiritual wisdom and understanding so that you may lead lives worthy of the Lord" (Col. 1:9-10 NRSV). By "spiritual understanding," Saint Paul means discerning, intuitive, and perceptive knowledge, usually found in solitude, the fruit of which is a profound insight into the *interconnectedness* of all things, through which we can situate ourselves in time and space to know God's will and do God's work in the world.

Discernment as "Seeing Through"

By exercising spiritual understanding, we come to see more clearly and hear more deeply the mysterious interconnectedness of all things (what the desert fathers called *theoria physike*—a vision of how things hang together). Discernment allows us to "see through" the appearance of things to their deeper meaning and come to know the interworkings of God's love and our unique place in the world. Discernment helps us come to know our true identity in creation, vocation in the world, and unique place in history as an expression of divine love.

Perceiving, seeing through, understanding, and being aware of God's presence are what is meant by discernment. Opening the heart to what is really and truly "there" is a fruit of contemplation and spiritual practice. Those who practice discernment are often more contemplative than those who are so active that they do not take the time to reflect on the inner meaning of appearances. The most interesting things in life often remain invisible to our ordinary senses, yet are visible to our spiritual perception. In large measure they can very easily be overlooked by the inattentive, busily distracted person that each of us can so easily become.

Contemplation looks not so much *at* things as *through* them, into their hearts, into their centers, and through their centers to discover the whole world of spiritual beauty, which is more real, has more mass and density, more energy and intensity, than physical matter in its coarser, cruder aspect. That is why the Greek fathers, who were great contemplatives, are known as the "diaretic fathers." (*Diarao* means "to see into," "to see through"—literally, into the heart of the matter.) That is why they could read the hearts and the troubled souls of those who consulted them: because they could see through appearances into the innermost self.

Jesus, of course, had this capacity to see truly. For example, Saint John tells us, "Jesus did not want to entrust himself to them because he *knew* what was in every heart" (John 2:24). Such intuitive and perceptive knowledge is the nature of discernment.

Discernment as "Being Seen"

I am struck by the way Jesus "saw" Nathanael under the tree in the Gospel of John. Even before meeting him, Jesus said of Nathanael: "Here is truly an Israelite in whom there is no deceit!" When the two men met on the road, Nathanael asked Jesus with amazement: "How do you *know* me?" Jesus answered him, "Before Philip called you, when you were under the fig tree, I *saw* you." Jesus's seeing through Nathanael under the fig tree was such a powerful act of discerning what was in his heart that it caused Nathanael to proclaim: "Rabbi, you are the Son of God! You are the King of Israel!" To which Jesus remarked, "You believe this because I told you I *saw* you under the fig tree? You will *see* greater things than these. . . . You will see heaven opened, and the angels of God ascending and descending upon the Son of Man" (John 1:47–51).

This wonderful story about seeing through to the heart of things raises a deeper question: Do I want to be fully seen by Jesus? Do I want to be known by him? If I do, then a faith can grow that will open my eyes to heaven and reveal Jesus as the Son of God. I will see great things when I am willing to be seen. I will receive new eyes that can see the mysteries of God's own life, but only when I allow God to see me, all of me, even those parts that I myself do not want to see.

While I was at the Abbey of the Genesee, I found that my anger and my desire to be special and to be admired all bubbled up in my times of solitude. I began to see how in so many ways I had been living for my own glory rather than for the greater glory of God.

Once we are willing to see and be seen by God, we can look

for signs of God's presence and guidance in every appearance presented to our senses. Discernment becomes a new way of seeing (and being seen) that results in divine revelation and direction. This heart knowledge enables us to lead a life worthy of the calling (Eph. 4:1).

The Purpose of Discernment

The purpose of discernment is to know God's will, that is, to find, *accept*, and *affirm* the unique way in which God's love is manifest in our life. To know God's will is to actively claim an intimate relationship with God, in the context of which we discover our deepest vocation and the desire to live that vocation to the fullest. It has nothing to do with passive submission to an external divine power that imposes itself on us. It has everything to do with active waiting on a God who waits for us.[4]

Finding ourselves in a relationship with God is prerequisite to discernment of God's will and direction. As in any relationship, there will be feelings of rejection as well as attraction, resentment as well as gratitude, fear as well as love. There will be ups and downs in faithfulness as we discover new things about ourselves and God. In our dynamic relationship with God, we can be sure of one thing: "If we are faithless, God is faithful still, for God cannot disown his own" (2 Tim. 2:13).

Acceptance of God's will does not mean submission or resignation to "whatever will be will be." Rather, we actively wait for the Spirit to move and prompt, and then discern what we are to do next. When we see ourselves in a relationship of love with God, there is always something of a lover's dilemma, a struggle to give and receive, to trust and obey the call.

REBORN IN THE SPIRIT

Jesus looked at the human condition with the eyes of love and tried to teach us how to look at ourselves and others "from above" and not "from below," where dark clouds obscure our vision. "I come from above," Jesus told his disciples, "and I want you to be reborn from above so that you will be able to see with new eyes" (John 3:3). This is what spiritual theology is all about—looking at reality with the eyes of God.

And there is so much to look at: land and skies; sun, moon, and stars; human beings in all their diversity; continents, countries, cities, and towns; events in the past, present, and future. That's why there are so many theologies. The sacred scriptures help us to look at the rich variety of all that is with the eyes of God, and so discern the way to live with more clarity of vision in the here and now.

Those who live lives worthy of their calling have been "reborn from above" and are able to see with the eyes of faith and hear with spiritual ears. Their lives of discernment are characterized by single-mindedness: they have but one true desire—to know God's heart and do God's will in all things. In the words of Jesus to Nicodemus, they live the truth and seek to "come to the light, so that it may be clearly seen that their deeds have been done in God" (John 3:21 NRSV). Such persons are so caught up in God's love that everything else can only receive its meaning and purpose in the context of that love. They ask only one question: "What is pleasing to the Spirit of God?" And as soon as they have heard the sound of the Spirit in the silence and solitude of their hearts, they follow its promptings even if it upsets their friends, disrupts their environment, and confuses their admirers.

People reborn in the Holy Spirit with spiritual understanding come across as very independent, not because of psychological training or individuation but because of the fruit of the Spirit which "blows where it chooses, and you hear the sound of it, but you do not know where it comes from or where it goes" (John 3:8). Spiritual rebirth is an evergreen openness to let the spirit of Jesus blow in us where it pleases.

Truly "born again" people always desire to be renewed continually, precisely because the Spirit keeps on revealing, in and around them, places of darkness that have not yet been transformed by the light. For as long as we live, we need to be reborn and deepen our spiritual understanding, as we walk together in the light.

DISCERNMENT IN SOLITUDE

Communion with God alone in prayer leads inevitably to community with God's people, and then to ministry in the world.[5] But it is good to begin this spiritual movement in solitude. Our first task in solitude is to simply allow ourselves to become aware of the divine presence, to "Be still, and know that I am God!" (Ps. 46:10). When we are alone with God, the Spirit prays in us. The challenge is to develop a simple discipline or spiritual practice to embrace some empty time and empty space every day.

When I went to the Abbey, I had begun to see Sunday as a special day, but all other days blurred into work and teaching. Through the sacred rhythm of the community prayers, I began to be pulled into a new way of perceiving time and a new way of experiencing God's presence. I was able to embrace solitude again, with all the disorienting and discouraging thoughts that intrude, as a royal road to God's presence. At first I spent most of my solitary time in the library, but increasingly, I was able to be alone before God in the quiet of my own room.

I encourage you to make a similar commitment to spending time alone with God each day for prayer and meditation. Biblical meditation is a traditional method of solitary prayer. By selecting a particular scripture verse from the gospel reading for the day, or a favorite psalm, or a sentence from a letter from Paul, you can create a safe wall around your heart that will allow you to pay attention. Reading and reciting a sacred text is not meant to fill up your empty space or limit your spiritual thoughts, but to set up boundaries around it. Sometimes it is helpful to take one word or phrase from the text and repeat it during your solitary prayer time. Some people find sitting quietly a good way to center their prayer. Others need to move and walk slowly to let the mind and body come into God's presence. Especially in the beginning, when you are easily distracted, it is good to be able to remember and repeat the word or phrase that attracted your attention. Then your focus and awareness can gradually descend from the mind into the heart and be held there for an extended period, close to the heart of God.[6]

Lectio divina,[7] or spiritual reading, is another helpful exercise to practice in solitude. By reading a biblical text three times and stopping to ponder the word, phrase, or image that calls our attention, we become more aware of the active presence of God's spirit within us. It is not reading to acquire new information or to learn a critical skill. Rather, it is a form of devotional reading in which we allow God to "read" us and respond to our deepest desire. Spiritual reading, therefore, is slow, deliberate, meditative reading in which we allow the words to penetrate our heart and question our spirit. *Lectio divina* means reading the Bible with reverence and openness to what the Spirit is saying to us in the present moment. Besides the Bible, many other books can be used for spiritual reading: classic Jewish and Christian devotional texts, contemporary essays on spiritual life, good theological reflections, spiritual autobiographies and lives of the saints, stories about new communities of faith, and so on. Most important is *how* we read—not to understand or control God, but to be understood and formed by God.

It is good to give some of our prayer time to intercession—to lift up to God particular people of whose pains and struggles we are aware, especially those with whom we live or work. People we pray for regularly come to receive a very special place in our heart and in the heart of God, and they are helped. Sometimes this happens immediately and sometimes over time. In addition, an inner community begins to grow in us, a community of love that strengthens us in our daily life. As a conclusion to our time of prayer, we can say the Lord's Prayer slowly. Or other prayers of the church and Christian tradition can be used. Such "formal" prayers connect us to the people of God and the whole of the praying church. I found at Genesee and in the following years that I often needed to pray from the newspapers, too. The tragedies and triumphs of the world were all part of the world for which I prayed.

The Spirit works deep within us, so deeply that we cannot always identify its presence. The effect of God's spirit is deeper than our thoughts and emotions. That is why setting aside a special time and place for prayer is so important. Often we do not feel like praying and our minds are distracted. The lack of motivation and difficulty focusing make us think that our prayer time is useless and wasted time. Still, it is very important to remain faithful to these times and simply stick with our promise to be with God, even if nothing in our minds, hearts, or bodies wants to be there. Simple faithfulness in prayer gives the Spirit of God a real chance to work in us, to help us be renewed in God's hands and be conformed to God's will. During these sacred times and places, we can be touched in deep, hidden, and tender places. We can become more fully aware of the divine presence and more open to God's guidance as we are led to new places of love.

Clock time can become sacred time. We can choose fifteen minutes, half an hour, or even a few hours, and set them aside for God. For a healthy physical, emotional, and spiritual life, we have to structure our time. We need to know beforehand when we will pray, when we will spend moments in spiritual reading, when we will participate in common worship, and so on. A rhythm of life in which sacred times and places are scheduled in gives us much spiritual support and causes us to look forward to them as "times of refreshing" for discernment.

DISCERNMENT IN COMMUNITY

While discernment begins in solitude, individual seekers of God always come together in community, for the Spirit gathers all believers into one body for accountability and mutual support. A person honestly seeking to know God's will and way will choose to be in community.

At the Abbey of the Genesee I began to see the utter necessity of life in community. I learned to bake bread, haul stones, and pray with the brothers. My capacity for intimacy with God was interrelated with my ability to love and live with the others in my community. Those months in the monastery taught me that the spiritual life is to be lived together. Since then I have sought to create community wherever I have lived. For the last few years, I have chosen to reside at Daybreak Community in Canada, where I live among the poor in spirit, to be spiritually formed, find support and accountability for my personal decisions, and be of service. Daybreak, as a L'Arche community, seeks to be a place where people with physical, emotional, and intellectual disabilities and their assistants live together as a sign of hope to the world. Daybreak, small and hidden as it is, wants to proclaim that love is stronger than fear, that joy is deeper than sorrow, that unity is more real than division, and that life is stronger than death. Being at Daybreak means being invited to make regular choices that radically contradict the powers and principalities of our world. We learn to discern by living out the challenge of the gospel together.

Living in Christian community offers concrete ways to make choices that support discernment—deep listening for the way and will of God. The choices we face often are quite specific and require thoughtful conversation around basic questions that confront our individual and collective motives and agendas: Are we working *with* the poor or choosing to *be* in solidarity with them? Are we squandering our time or seizing time as a constant opportunity to discover more about ourselves, our neighbors, and our God? Are we structuring our days to be distracted and entertained, or to let our hearts grow more mature and strong? Are we responding to our inner fears and pains by ignoring them, or do we choose to face them and live into and through our fears and pains with the help of others who accompany us? Are we talking or praying, worrying or giving thanks, looking at images that arouse or those that bring joy, dwelling with our anger or with the one who can bring peace?

All these questions show that we are constantly making choices that can lead us toward God's way and will. These decisions are difficult because we live in a world that thinks we are wasting our time, that there are more exciting ways to use our talents, that there is more money to be made, more prestige, education, and success to be had, more respect and honor to gain, if we would just step away from our spiritual idealism and be realistic in our choices like everyone else.

CONCRETE SUGGESTIONS FOR DISCERNMENT IN COMMUNITY

Specific spiritual practices form a context and structure for discernment in community, in different seasons of the liturgical year, as well as in critical moments of our daily journey of faith. While few guidelines can be given that are good for every person or community of faith, the following concrete suggestions based on practices at the Daybreak Community may be helpful in other faith communities.

Sacred Time and Space

The first task of a faith community is to create sacred time and space, when and where we can allow God to reshape our hearts and lives and communities. Community offers sacred times (a regular schedule for worship, prayer, fasting, scripture reading, and fellowship) and sacred space (chapels, sanctuaries, retreats, homes, and nature) to take a step back from the urgencies and emergencies of our busy lives and listen to God and to each other as children of God. The Daybreak community, for example, has a chapel and retreat center that invite us to be quiet and peaceful, to rest and be restored, to read about the spiritual life, to share our journey with others, to worship in private or common prayer. It is a good place to come together for teaching or workshops, to share in small groups for spiritual formation, to seek individual spiritual direction, or to practice spiritual discernment, and just to become more open to God's presence.

Community Worship

Worship at L'Arche Daybreak is centered in the chapel, a simple, accessible building full of color and light. The community gathers daily in the chapel for Eucharist and common prayer. People from all walks of life and from very different religious traditions share their unique spiritual gifts and offer their particular forms of worship, as well as developing new forms and common ways of worship. Together, we bring our joys and pains, share our smiles and shed our tears, and open our hearts to God. We listen to the Word of God and to words of encouragement, warning, and hope. Thus in worship the chapel becomes a holy dwelling and a special place for formation and discernment. Sitting in silence after we have prayed together, we listen for God to speak.

In common worship (service of the Word and Sacrament), we avoid busyness and entertainment. We gather to be made into a spiritual body in which God's presence can be made manifest. We sing, read, dance, sit in silence, and pray, allowing our liturgical actions to open space among us where God can act. We try to do nothing in haste, allowing for silence and encouraging simplicity.

Spiritual Teaching

Communities of faith intrinsically offer informal and formal teaching on the spiritual life. We have found that there is great value in being exposed to classic and contemporary biblical scholarship and theological reflection, to the different schools of spirituality, to historical spiritual writers, and to contemporary issues of justice and the spiritual life. We encourage all members of the community to bring their ideas, to share their perspectives on the Bible, and to tell stories from their own lives. It is important for people who have little time for systematic reading and study but who still long for a deeper understanding of their lives and work to have opportunities for sound teaching and spiritual formation. Without seeing the larger context of their lives, the danger exists that some will lose touch with the spiritual roots and theological traditions of their community of faith. Good teaching affects one's personal prayer life, common worship, the desire for spiritual reading, and thus the practice of discernment. To want to know God's plan and purpose without regular prayer and engagement with scripture and God's people is like trying to bake a cake without assembling the various ingredients. Discernment grows out of the life of faith rooted in community.

Such are the gifts of Christian community: listening, sharing, worship, prayer, music, books, images, ways of resting and eating, walking and talking, laughing and crying—sacred time and space set apart to "taste and see that the Lord is good" (Ps. 34:8 NRSV).

A New Way of Seeing

When Christian community provides sacred space and times for discernment, we will gradually be lifted up into God's dwelling place and come to see ourselves, our neighbors, and our world in a new light. This "seeing" does not require intellectual knowledge, articulated insight, or a concrete opinion. No, it is a sharing in the knowledge of God's heart, a deeper wisdom, a new way of living and loving.

Discernment reveals new priorities, directions, and gifts from God. We come to realize that what previously seemed so important for our lives, loses its power over us. Our desire to be successful, well liked, and influential becomes increasingly less important as we come closer to God's heart. To our surprise, we even may experience a strange inner freedom to follow a new call or direction as previous concerns move into the background of our consciousness. We begin to see the beauty of the small and hidden life that Jesus lived in Nazareth. Most rewarding of all is the discovery that as we pray more each day, God's will—that is, God's concrete ways of loving us and our world—gradually is made known to us.

Giving God a Chance

Spiritual discernment comes from the Spirit of God. The human side is the concentrated effort to create sacred time and empty space, as well as concrete structures and boundaries, where God can speak to us.

Christian community offers unique opportunities for spiritual formation and discernment. Together, we are called to let God become the center of our lives, speak to us, guide us, hold us, renew us deep within. We have the freedom to say yes to God's call and to choose to live it in very specific ways. Our communities help us make and sustain that choice. Thus God has a real chance to form us into lights in the darkness, a source of hope for many in the world. That, after all, is the true goal of spiritual discernment.

Discernment is rooted in spiritual practice, yet it is not a step-by-step process. It requires learning to listen for and recognize over time the voice and character of God in our hearts and daily lives. In the next chapter we will look at what Saint Paul calls "the discernment of spirits." Learning to listen to the Spirit demands sorting what is of God in our lives and what is not.

EXERCISES FOR DEEPER DISCERNMENT

1. Discernment is about seeing, knowing, and being known. Do you want to be seen by God? Do you want to be truly known, with all your inner thoughts and outer activities laid out before an all-seeing, all-knowing God? Write a personal letter to God openly and honestly looking at the areas of life you are not sure you want God to investigate. Of course, God knows these things already. This is an exercise for you to see what areas of your life you might want to keep private. Once you identify them, pray that God will help you see yourself (and these tender areas) fully as God sees you.

2. People who are "reborn from above" (John 3:7) are those who seek to do what is pleasing to the Spirit of God. Make a list of all the activities and desires of your heart that you believe are pleasing to God. Try to write a poem or hymn of praise or gratitude for all God's goodness that overflows into your life.

3. Define your spiritual community. Who is allowed to know you and hold you accountable? If you have identified people who know you at a soul level, take a moment to write them

a note of thanks for their role in your life. If you did not identify persons who have free range in your life to lift you up and encourage you, begin to pray about who to cultivate as a spiritual companion and how to do it. Discernment performed alone often can become delusion. We need each other.

4. What shared practices (meditation, prayer, songs, Eucharist, silence, service in the world) are your most natural pathways to listening to God in your daily life? Reflect on the times when you discerned God's presence. What were you doing? Where were you? What insight might these reflections give you about your need for sacred time and sacred space?

TWO

Distinguishing Spirits of Truth and Falsehood

Discernment of spirits is a lifelong task. I can see no other way for discernment than to be committed to a life of unceasing prayer and contemplation, a life of deep communion with the Spirit of God.

—*Henri Nouwen in Gracias!, p. 13*

While on retreat at the Abbey of the Genesee, I read about vices and virtues and how to subdue the powers of evil and embrace the powers of good in *The Ladder of Divine Ascent* by John Climacus. In my prayerful reading, I found myself pondering the following words:

If some [monks] are still dominated by their former bad habits, and yet can teach by mere words, let them [continue to] teach. But they should not have authority as well. For, perhaps, being put to shame by their own words, they will eventually begin to practice what they preach.

This graceful provision in the midst of a stern book offers both consolation and warning, but most of all it seems to summarize my own story and concern: How can I better practice what I teach and preach? How do I overcome my own inconsistencies and teach about the spiritual life both by words and example? Yet even when I fail to practice what I teach or am put to shame by my own words, might my struggle to free myself from the "law of the flesh" and to live according to the "ways of the Spirit" be helpful to others with similar conflicts? John of the Ladder points out that even those who are "stuck in the mire and the mud" have something to teach others:

Bogged down as they were, they were telling passers-by how they had sunk there, explaining this for their salvation, so that they should not fall in the same way. However, for the salvation of others, the all-powerful God delivered them too from the mud.[1]

As I reflect on my life today, many years after my ordination to the priesthood and that season of monastic life at the Abbey of Genesee, I still feel like the least of God's holy people. Looking back over the years, I realize that I am still struggling with the same problems I had all those years ago. Notwithstanding my many prayers, periods of retreat, advice from friends, and time with counselors and confessors, it seems that very little, if anything, has changed. I am still the restless, nervous, intense, distracted, and impulse-driven person I was when I set out on this spiritual journey. I am still searching for inner peace and unity and a resolution to my many internal conflicts. At times this obvious lack of spiritual maturation depresses me as I enter into the "mature" years. The struggle Saint Paul describes so well in his Letter to the Romans is my story as well: "I do not understand my own actions. For I do not do what I want, but I do the very thing I hate. . . . I can will what is right, but I cannot do it. . . . So I find it to be a law that when I want to do what is good, evil lies close at hand. For I delight in the law of God in my inmost self, but I see in my [flesh] another law at war with the law of my mind."

So, "who will rescue me?" I pray with Saint Paul. "Thanks be to God through Jesus Christ our Lord!" (Rom. 7:15–25 NRSV).

DISTINGUISHING SPIRITS

I am aware of my tendency to divide people into good ones and evil ones, as if I could see into people's hearts and know for sure why they act the way they do. But I understand that we are all touched by evil and limitation and all need mercy and grace. Knowing that all people and situations have multiple motives and choices, it is necessary to learn how to discern spirits.

Discernment is not about judging other people's motives. It's about distinguishing good guidance from harmful messages, and the Holy Spirit from evil spirits. This essential sorting, known as *discernment of spirits,* is intended for our protection and not for our judgment.

Discernment (Gr. *diakriseis,* spiritual judgment, understanding, assessment, estimation, or separation) is both a gift and a spiritual discipline. The New Testament concept is found in Romans 12:2, 1 Corinthians 1:19; 4:4; 11:29; 11:31; 12:10, and Hebrews 4:12. The phrase *discernment of spirits* occurs in three New Testament texts: in 1 Corinthians 12:10 as one of the gifts of the Spirit; in Hebrews 5:14 as an exercise of the spiritually mature "whose faculties have been trained by practice to distinguish good from evil;" and in Romans 14:1 as a reminder to "accept the one who is weak in faith, but not for the purpose of passing judgment on his opinions." Taken together, discernment is a spiritual capacity for distinguishing or discriminating between opposing forces. "For the flesh sets its desire against the Spirit, and the Spirit against the flesh; for these are in opposition to one another, so that you may not do the things that you please" (Gal. 5:17, NASB).

The one who practices discernment is able to distinguish whether a particular action or message is from the Spirit of God and to assess whether someone is speaking truth or falsehood. Though it is presented by Saint Paul as an individual spiritual gift, as with all gifts, it is to be practiced in community.

Discernment of spirits is a lifelong task. I can see no other path to discernment than to be committed to a life of unceasing prayer and contemplation, a life of deep communion with the Spirit of God. Such a life will slowly develop in us an inner sensitivity, enabling us to distinguish between the law of the flesh and the law of the Spirit.

When I was nearing my fiftieth birthday, I traveled to Bolivia to learn Spanish. I was again seeking to clarify my vocational calling. Was I to keep teaching the bright, successful students in the seminary or was I being called to live among the poor? There I struggled to discern the spirits I sensed in daily life. I remember feeling surrounded by destructive powers one day in Cochabamba. I knew from experience that my sensitivity to what scripture calls "powers and principalities" was stronger some days than others. As I biked through downtown, I saw groups of young men loitering on street corners waiting for the next movie to start. I stopped and walked through a bookstore stacked with magazines depicting violence, sex, and gossip, endless forms of provocative advertisement and unnecessary articles imported from other parts of the world. I had the dark feeling of being surrounded by powers much greater than myself and felt the seductive allure of sin all around me. I got a glimpse of the evil behind all the horrendous realities that plague our world— extreme hunger, nuclear weapons, torture, exploitation, rape, child abuse, and various forms of oppression—and how they all have their small and sometimes unnoticed beginnings in the human heart. The demon is patient in the way it seeks to devour and destroy the work of God. I felt intensely the darkness of the world around me.

After a period of aimless wandering, I biked to a small Carmelite convent close to the house of my hosts. A very friendly Carmelite sister spoke to me and invited me into the chapel to pray. She radiated joy, peace, and, yes, light. She told me about the light that shines into the darkness without saying a word about it. As I looked around, I saw images of Teresa of Avila and Thérèse of Lisieux, two saints who taught in their own times that God speaks in subtle ways and that peace and certainty follow when we hear well. Suddenly, it seemed to me that these two saints were talking to me about another world, another life, another love. As I knelt down in the small and simple chapel, I knew that this place was filled with God's presence. Because of the prayers offered there day and night, the chapel was a place of light, and the spirit of darkness had not gotten a foothold there.

My visit to the Carmelite convent helped me realize again that where evil seems to hold sway, God is not far away, and where God shows his presence, evil may not remain absent very long. There always remains a choice to be made between the creative power of love and life and the destructive power of hatred and death. I, too, must make that choice myself, again and again. Nobody else, not even God, will make that choice for me.

Upon reflection, it became increasingly clear to me that I know quite well the difference between darkness and light but do not always have the courage to name them by their true names. There is a strong temptation to deal with the darkness as if it

were light, and with the light as if it were darkness. Knowing
Jesus, reading his words, and praying create increasing clarity
about evil and good, sin and grace, Satan and God. This clarity
calls me to choose the way to the light fearlessly and straightfor-
wardly. The transparent life is a life in which heart, mind, and
gut are united in choosing the light.

Resisting the Darkness

What is the greatest temptation? Money, sex, power? They seem
to be the obvious ones, and we are easily caught by one or all of
them. In the monastic traditions, vows of poverty, celibacy, and
obedience are intended to help monks and nuns resist the temptations of money, sex, and power and to follow the way of Jesus.
But over the years I have come to the conclusion that the greatest
and most destructive temptation may not be any of these three.
I wonder if the greatest temptation is self-rejection. Could it be
that beneath all the lures to greed, lust, and success rests a great
fear of never being enough or not being lovable?

Instead of taking a careful look at the circumstances or trying
to understand my own and others' limitations without rejection or judgment, when I fall into temptation, I tend to blame
myself—not just for what I did but for who I am. My dark side
says, "I am no good. I deserve to be pushed aside, forgotten, rejected, and abandoned." Self-rejection is the greatest enemy of
the spiritual life because it contradicts the sacred voice that calls
us God's beloved. Being the beloved expresses the core truth of
our existence.[2]

How do I discern the voice that says "be humble" from the one
that says "you're nothing"? Humility has nothing to do with self-
rejection. You can only be humble if you have a deep self-respect.
Self-rejection cannot form the basis of a humble life. It leads only
to complaints, jealousy, anger, and even violence. It is a most

dangerous temptation. I know this from my own experience. Every time I start to experience myself as worthless or useless, a "nobody," I know I am on the slippery slope to isolation and dark emotions.

I know that I give hope to others only when I have found that hope in the midst of my own despair. At times I find myself so deeply pulled into my own darkness that hope escapes me. How can I speak heart to heart about hope when I am still a victim of my own despair? I am so little in control of my feelings and emotions! Often I have to just let them pass through me and trust that they won't hang around too long.

I have found that Saint Teresa's call to focus on the goodness of God when I need to discern helps me fight the demons of despair, self-rejection, and fear, and has overcome the powers of darkness with the power of God many times. I have often prayed the prayer of Saint Teresa, "*Solo Dios basta,* God alone is enough," when I have needed to discern whether what I was hearing and experiencing was of God or not. Praying these words slowly and out loud can help me enter into God's presence, where there is peace and certainty that God is always with me and loves me.

> Let nothing disturb you
> Let nothing frighten you.
> Those who cling to God
> will lack nothing
> Let nothing disturb you
> Let nothing frighten you
> God alone is enough.[3]

FINDING THE LIGHT

Resisting the forces of evil and death is possible only when we are fully in touch with the forces of goodness and life. When I try to confront the powers of darkness directly, I often feel so power-less that I lose contact with the source of my own life. How easy it is to become a victim of the very forces I am fighting against! When all my attention goes to protesting death, death itself may end up receiving more attention than it deserves. There is wisdom from the fourth-century monks of the Egyptian desert: "Do not combat the demons directly." The wise ones of the desert felt that a direct confrontation with the forces of evil required such spiritual maturity that few would be ready for it. Instead of paying so much attention to the prince of darkness, they advised their disciples to focus on the Lord of light, and thus, indirectly but inevitably, thwart the power of darkness.

In the midst of our darkness and vulnerability to fear and despair, Saint John of the Cross, a spiritual friend of Teresa's, writes of a light too bright for our eyes to see. We may not be able to look directly into its brightness, yet in this divine light we find the source of our being. In this light we live, even when we cannot grasp it. The light sets us free to resist all evil and to be faithful in the darkness, always waiting for the day when God's presence will be revealed to us in all its glory.

I know from experience that I cannot always find the light, or walk in the light of God, alone. I need the love and support of my brothers and sisters in the community of faith. My own spiritual life has been unthinkable without the intercessory prayers of others. Many crucial decisions needed to be taken, many classes needed to be taught, many promises needed to be fulfilled, and at the same time I have often felt so tired, so heavy of heart, and so melancholic that I wondered how I would ever be able to live through that time. I couldn't pray. Not only was I unable to find time to step into the light, but even when I had time I found no inner rest. The prayers I said often felt empty and useless. During one such period of trying to discern between the good I wanted to do and the pull to just give in to self-rejection and darkness, I decided to write to twelve friends, whose love for me was as real

as their prayers, and asked them to pray for me ẹ̣
coming month. I explained to them my spiritual ἀ
inner fears. It didn't take long to experience sometḥ
though my own prayers remained painfully barren, ̣ ̣ ̣ ̣ ̣ ̣ ̣ felt
surrounded by a network of prayerful support. I knew I belonged
to a spiritual family who lifted me up to God, and I sensed that I
was part of an active community of prayer. It felt as though others
were praying in my place and I didn't have to worry.

A task that seemed impossible to fulfill proved possible, people
whom I feared might judge me proved to be friends, and deep
temptations that had seemed insurmountable proved to be temporary distractions. During that month, I kept feeling the real
presence of my praying friends. Now I know better than ever that
the prayers surrounding me give me life.

Help from Praying to Saints

Beyond the strength I received from friends who remembered
to pray for me during a fearful time, I also have experienced a
special closeness to certain saints or holy ones in the church's
memory who speak to me of faithful witness and strength, sometimes providing guidance in time of need. In times of struggle, I
do not hesitate to ask them to pray for me, as they encourage me
to practice discernment and live a spiritual life.

Although we tend to think of saints as holy and pious, pictur-
ing them with halos above their heads and ecstatic gazes, true
saints are much more accessible. Whether they are still living or
have joined the "great cloud of witnesses," they are available to
help us in time of need. Saints are men and women like us, who
live ordinary lives and struggle with ordinary problems. What
makes them saints is their clear and unwavering focus on God
and God's people. The saints are our brothers and sisters, calling
us to become like them.

The apostle Paul speaks about all those who belong to Christ as "holy people" or "saints." He directs his letters to "those who have been consecrated in Christ Jesus and called to be God's holy people" (see 1 Cor. 1:2; see also Eph. 1:1). As saints, we belong to that large network of God's people that shines like a multitude of stars in the dark sky of the universe.

Belonging to the communion of saints means being connected with all people transformed by the Spirit of Jesus. This connection is deep and intimate. It is a family of people set apart by God to provide light in the darkness. It embraces people from long ago and far away. Those who have lived as brothers and sisters of Jesus continue to live within us even though they have died, just as Jesus continues to live within us even though *he* has died.

It has always fascinated me that some people—so-called saints or holy people—never really leave us when they die. Their deaths somehow free them from the constraints of earthly existence and bring them closer to more people than they could ever have known on earth. God continues to speak to us through their lives, deaths, and memory so as to draw us close.

Saints are people who become our neighbors in a new way when they enter into the glory of God. The French word for neighbor is *prochain*—someone who is *proche,* which means "close." Those who have lived so fully in the Spirit of Jesus can draw close and guide us, both in life and death. They become new *prochains* through their death. Thérèse of Lisieux, for example, was hardly known during her lifetime but is now a close neighbor to many who follow her example of a holy life. And so it is with Saint Francis, Saint Benedict, and Saint Ignatius of Loyola. The same is true for many holy men and women who may never be canonized by the church—such as Oscar Romero, Dorothy Day, Marthe Robin, and many whose names we will never know—but who lived among us as neighbors and now *prochains* through their death.

THE INTERCESSIONS OF MARTHE ROBIN

Have you ever prayed in a place where a great battle between good and evil, light and darkness, had been fought? I felt it in a chapel in Bolivia—that the very chapel where I prayed had been prepared by the faithful ones who had prayed there before me. I again experienced it while praying in a place readied for discerning, when I first visited the home of Marthe Robin (1902–81), who was born, lived, and died in a simple farmhouse on a hill not far from the small town of Châteauneuf-de-Galaure in France.

I visited the L'Arche community in Trosly, France, in 1984. The founder, Jean Vanier's mother, had told me about Marthe Robin—an unusual twentieth-century saint who somehow experienced in her own body some of the physical pain and suffering of Jesus. She is remembered worldwide and became one of the most important spiritual guides during the year I lived at L'Arche. As I knelt in her small, dark room, in which only a small lamp allowed me to identify the different objects, I had a feeling of being in a place where the great battle of Jesus was fought by one of his followers. I was at the place where a simple peasant woman had to choose— every second of her life— between good and evil, God and Satan, life and death. I suddenly knew in a new way what Saint Paul meant when he said:

> Put on the whole armor of God, so that you may be able to stand against the wiles of the devil. For our struggle is not against enemies of blood and flesh, but against the rulers, against the authorities, against the cosmic powers of this present darkness, against the spiritual forces of evil in the heavenly places. Therefore take up the whole armor of God so that you may be able to withstand on that evil day, having done everything, to stand firm. (Eph. 6:11–13 NRSV)

After praying there once, I decided to return often and to pray there longer and more deeply. Now Marthe is one of the most important guides in my life. Thinking about her life and praying where she often prayed help me resist evil and seek divine wisdom.

I find it easier to pray in places where people have prayed long before, and harder to pray in places where seldom a prayer has been uttered. This is important to me, since I move around quite a bit. In an empty train compartment, a hotel room, or even a quiet study, there often seems to be a spirit that holds me back. I could have stayed and prayed for many hours in Marthe's room. Seldom have I felt such inner peace. Let me tell you some of her unusual story. Her life is one example from the lives of the faithful, which show how one can live a life of prayer that leads to discerning good from harm.

In 1918, a young Marthe Robin became aware of her vocation to live her life in full solidarity with the sufferings of Jesus. In 1926, her parents thought she was going to die of a strange disease. Marthe experienced Saint Thérèse of Lisieux appearing to her three times, telling her not only that she would live but that she was called to continue in her life the mission of Saint Thérèse in the world. Soon after these apparitions, Marthe became paralyzed. As she was no longer able to move her arms or legs, her parents put her on a small divan bed, where she remained until her death more than five decades later.

In 1930, she told others that she heard Jesus ask, "Do you want to be like me in all things?" It was an invitation to experience not only the physical pain Jesus endured during his passion but also the immense suffering of his heart. Marthe answered a simple yes to that divine invitation.

Every week from Thursday night until Monday during this period, she focused on living in solidarity with the agony of Jesus at Gethsemane on his way to Calvary, his death on the cross, and the joy of his resurrection. On Tuesdays and Wednesdays, she received visitors and spoke to them in a very simple, childlike way about their lives, calling them to conversion and communicating to them what Jesus wanted them to do. She told some to start Christian schools for boys and girls, and others to start retreat centers or small communities, which are still in existence. She also received many letters from people asking for her guidance and intercession.

On February 10, 1936, Marthe had the following conversation with a visiting priest, Father George Finet. According to this account, Martha was a visionary woman who suffered greatly and was able to discern on behalf of others.

"Reverend, God has asked me to tell you something: You have to come to Châteauneuf to start the first Foyer de Charité [retreat house]."

Totally surprised, Père Finet answered, "But I am not of this diocese."

"What does that matter, when God wants it?"

"Oh, excuse me. I hadn't thought of that! But what am I to do there?"

"A lot of things, especially retreats."

"But I do not know how to do that."

"You will learn."

"Retreats for three days?"

"No, since one cannot change a soul in three days, God asks for five days."

"What to do during these five days? Discussions? Sharing?"

"No . . . complete silence."

"Complete silence? But how can I require such silence of women and girls?"

"Because God asks for it."

"But how to make these retreats known?"

"You must not say anything. God will bring all the retreatants to you."

I confirmed this conversation with Father Finet, who at eighty-four years was willing to give me a tour of the first retreat house built during World War II in Châteauneuf-de-Galaure near Marthe's home. Today there are fifty-seven of these retreat centers spread all over the world, offering spiritual retreats for adults. What began as a conversation became a worldwide retreat movement for the spiritual formation of the laity. Hundreds of laypersons are working full-time in these retreat houses to help people discover their gifts and the mystery of God's redemptive presence in the world. Because Marthe discerned God's desire for such a mission, she passed on divine instructions to an open and faithful priest.

I suspect some of you are tempted to read quickly past this section. It is easy to dismiss the example of those who suffered greatly and prayed fervently in the past as people who do not know what it is like to follow God and experience temptations today. But in Marthe's life is the desire to let God live through her. She offered her very body as a vessel for God to speak through.[4]

Just as praying with Saint Teresa helped me focus on God's goodness, I found a prayer of Marthe Robin's that gave me words to move from being in the presence of God to surrendering my life to God's guidance, even in times of suffering and confusion:

May God take my memory and all it remembers,
Take my heart and all its affections,
Take my intelligence and all its powers;
May they only serve your greatest glory.
Take my will completely,
for always I empty it out in yours.
No longer what I want, O my sweetest Jesus,
but always what you want!
Take me . . . receive me . . . direct me.
Guide me! I surrender and abandon myself to you!
I surrender myself to you as a small sacrifice of

Love, of praise and Gratitude, for the Glory of your Holy
Name,

for the enjoyment of your Love, the triumph of your Sacred
Heart,

and for the perfect fulfillment of your Designs in me and
around me.[5]

JESUS AND HIS SAINTS

Jesus, of course, is the supreme guide on living in the presence of
God. Jesus's death and resurrection brought him so close to his
disciples that they could live not only *with* him but also *in* him
and *through* him. The sending of the Spirit of Jesus at Pentecost
allowed disciples to come closer to him than they ever could
before his death, and to receive guidance through the Spirit.
We can, too. By learning to be sensitive to the powers of light
and darkness in our hearts and in our world, we can find places
that help us pray where the faithful have prayed before us. We
can pray words that they have given us when we are at a loss for
words, and we can live close to our neighbors in faith, both the
living and those we know through books, letting them speak into
our lives words of guidance.

EXERCISES FOR DEEPER DISCERNMENT

1. Nouwen looked back at his life and saw that he had some
   persistent challenges which he had struggled with for years.
   He remained a restless, nervous, intense, distracted, and
   impulse-driven person. Retreats and prayers did not help
   these struggles to subside. Still, he found freedom in trusting that God loved him, would guide him, and would allow

him to offer guidance to others even when these challenges were not removed. Can you name the persistent challenges in your life that keep you in need of discernment and guidance? How have those very challenges allowed you to be of assistance to others?

2. In a period of discernment when away from home in Bolivia, Nouwen fled to a small chapel to seek peace and help when he sensed the overwhelming darkness of provocative media and futile distractions as tempting him away from hearing God's voice. Where do you flee or go when you are overwhelmed with a sense of darkness or confusion? This chapel, and later Marthe Robin's room, became sanctuaries of peace where Nouwen went to pray for guidance. Where do you go? If you don't know, how might you seek out a refuge that has been well prepared by others' prayers?

3. Nouwen relied on words prayed by others, like Saint Thérèse and Marthe Robin, in times of temptation and despair. What prayers or scriptures do you rely on when you don't have your own words or the darkness seems especially impenetrable? Experiment with one of the prayers in this chapter. Feel free to adapt them as your own.

4. The guidance Nouwen received from his experience follows a general pattern: when aware of darkness and the need to discern, find a refuge where you can pray knowing others have prayed there, too; focus your prayers on the goodness and light of God rather than the darkness; let others intercede for you; and find some "neighbors" in faith, whether living or dead, who can serve as guides for living faithfully in times of suffering and confusion. Does this pattern resonate with your experience? If not, can you identify your own lessons from discerning in the past? It can be helpful to

understand how God's guidance has reached you in periods of darkness when you discerned the way to walk and live.

5. Suggested passage for *lectio divina:* 1 John 1:1–10.

6. Prayer of the Psalmist: "I am your servant; O, God, grant me discernment, that I may understand your statutes" (Ps. 119:125).

PART TWO

Discerning Guidance in Books, Nature, People, and Events

THREE

Read the Way Forward

God speaks to us all the time and in many ways,
but it requires spiritual discernment
to hear God's voice, see what God sees,
and read the signs in daily life.
                    —Henri Nouwen

No one can discern the signs of daily life alone. We turn to our
religious traditions and also to the wisdom others have gained
and recorded from their own journeys. That is why most people
turn to books and other types of reading when seeking to discover God's way forward. Reading often means gathering information, acquiring new insight and knowledge, and mastering a
new field. It can lead to degrees, diplomas, and certificates. Spiritual reading, however, is different. It means not simply reading

about spiritual things but also reading about spiritual things in a spiritual way. That requires a willingness not just to read but to be read, not just to master but to be mastered by words. As long as we read the Bible or a spiritual book simply to acquire knowledge, our reading does not help us in our spiritual life.

We can become very knowledgeable about spiritual matters without becoming truly spiritual people. As we learn to read spiritually about spiritual things, we open our hearts to God's voice. Discernment requires not only reading with the heart but being willing to put down the book we are reading to just listen to what God is saying to us through its words.

I want to share with you what I learned from Thomas Merton, one of the important spiritual pioneers of the last century, about reading the signs of God's guidance in books. By telling you about some of Merton's influences and interpretations, as well as my own, I hope to show you how reading from the wise ones who lived before or who live alongside you can help you find your way home.

SIGNS OF GOD'S DIRECTION

When I met Thomas Merton on a short retreat at Gethsemane Abbey in 1967, I felt a deep affinity with the man I had admired for so long through his writings. While he made a huge impression on me, the influence was all in one direction.[1] Still, I wrote a book in Dutch on Merton's approach to the spiritual life, and what I know about reading the signs of daily life I learned from him. Merton is still a model for me on how to find God's guidance in books, including what monks and mystics call "the book of Nature." He also witnessed to me about how to read the people placed in your path, as well as events and signs of the times. God is always speaking to us, but it requires spiritual discernment to hear God's voice, see what God sees, and read the signs in daily life.

In heeding a call to break with his past and leave the secular world behind to live inside the walls of the Trappist abbey in Kentucky, Thomas Merton chose a difficult path. He believed various signs had brought him there. The books he read, experiences in nature, people he met along the way, and critical events in his own life and in the world made spiritual impressions on him as a young man seeking guidance. For us as well, paying attention to the signs in daily life provides a starting place for a deeper and more systematic discernment and spiritual reflection. When we ask, as Merton did, "What of God is being revealed in this book or in this experience?" we are led to new insight and to ways of saying yes to God's direction in our lives.

HOW GOD SPEAKS THROUGH BOOKS

The sixteenth-century saint and founder of the Jesuits, Ignatius of Loyola, was converted to Christ by reading books about the lives of the saints. I can understand why, because every time I read the life of a saint I experience a powerful call to be as loving and devoted as that holy one of God was in life. But it is not just canonized saints that call us to conversion, or the "cloud of witnesses" who touch our spiritual lives. All who faithfully live the Christian life—whether still living or in memory—can exercise a deep and positive influence on our spiritual lives. Reading short biographies of people like Ignatius of Loyola, Mother Teresa of Calcutta, Francis of Assisi, Thérèse of Lisieux, John of the Cross, Teresa of Avila, Brother Lawrence, Brother Roger of Taizé, or any of God's faithful servants, is like stepping out of this world and back into it again under the guidance of these special men and women. They all know the struggles I know, but they are living with them in a different way.

Jean-Pierre de Caussade, more than two hundred years after his death, still speaks to me about what he called the "sacrament of the present moment." In his little book on prayer, he assures us that God is speaking and revealing his will in every moment of every day, and that we can discern God's presence and guidance through simple prayers each day: "When we abandon ourselves to God in prayer, then each moment becomes a sacrament of joy, gratitude, and loving acceptance of the will of God manifest in that moment."[2] Likewise, the example and spiritual legacy of Brother Lawrence in the late seventeenth century continues to help me "pray without ceasing" by recognizing with gratitude God's presence in the ordinary activities and routines of each day.[3]

BOOKS AND WRITERS THAT
LED MERTON TO GOD

Here's what Thomas Merton wrote as the first sentence of his autobiography, *The Seven Storey Mountain:* "On the last day of January 1915, under the sign of the Water Bearer, in the year of a great war and down in the shadow of some French mountains on the borders of Spain, I came into the world."[4] Just that sentence shows that we all must discern our core identity in the midst of the times in which we live. For so many years he felt like an orphan, constantly traveling around France, England, and the United States and never feeling at home in the world. It is not surprising that he sought a safe place in the monastery, where he could feel at home—a spiritually grounded place that might bring order to the endless series of opposing ideas, and an aesthetically enriching place where books, as well religious images and art, would continue to speak to him of God. Everything he read, saw, and experienced imposed the larger question, What can I say yes to, without reserve?

When Merton entered as a student in Columbia University in 1935, he was already very well read and familiar with the literary classics, to which his godfather had introduced him in his previous London milieu. Ernest Hemingway, James Joyce, D. H. Lawrence, Evelyn Waugh, and Graham Greene had become familiar names to him. His early diaries are filled with critical commentary on books by William Blake, Saint Augustine, Saint Thomas, and Dante. He read widely to feed his intellect but also to find companions on the journey. Two volumes of philosophy, especially, brought him to a deeper level of knowledge than the London literary circle could offer: *The Spirit of Medieval Philosophy* by Etienne Gilson, and *Ends and Means* by Aldous Huxley.

One of the life-directing ideas he learned from Gilson was the scholastic concept of *aseitas*[5]—that God is pure being, non-contingent and independent of any act of existing, which he describes in *The Seven Storey Mountain* as a vigorous and compelling attribute of God:

> In this one word, which can be applied to God alone, and which expresses his most characteristic attribute, I discovered an entirely new concept of God—a concept which showed me at once that the belief of Catholics was by no means the vague and rather superstitious hangover from an unscientific age that I had believed it to be. On the contrary, here was a notion of God that was at the same time deep, precise, simple and accurate and, what is more, charged with implications which I could not even begin to appreciate, but which I could at least dimly estimate, even with my own lack of philosophical training.[6]

The concept of God as pure, necessary, and Supreme Being, foundation of all life and source of all existence, and not just the anthropomorphic grandfatherly figure in the sky, delighted Merton and called him to deeper theological reflection on Christian mysticism. Grounded in a firm foundation of scholastic philosophical theology, Merton felt confident in exploring the frontiers of spirituality in the writings of a wide variety of spiritual seekers from Meister Eckhart and Chuang Tzu to the Zen Buddhists, Hindus, and Muslim Sufis.[7]

Another author Merton greatly appreciated was Aldous Huxley, whose *Ends and Means* brought him into contact with Eastern mysticism. Merton says Huxley "had read widely and deeply and intelligently in all kinds of Christian and Oriental mystical literature, and had come out with the astonishing truth that all this, far from being a mixture of dreams and magic and charlatanism, was very real and very serious."[8] Huxley, to his surprise, also transformed Merton's understanding of asceticism (self-denial). "If we want to live differently from wild beasts, we must free the spirit by means of prayer and asceticism," Huxley concluded. The word *asceticism* had up to then meant a twisting of nature through denying what seemed to be human desires, but Huxley showed him that only through asceticism can the spirit know itself and find God. Merton shrank from this but still began hesitatingly to sense the Spirit leading him in this way.

FOLLOWING MERTON

What prompted Merton to follow the ascetical path of self-knowledge leading to experiential knowledge of God in the heart, I am sure, is the same spiritual insight that I came to in reading some of the books that most influenced Merton. Following his lead, I read all I could on both Western and Eastern mysticism, especially the mystical Christian tradition on asceticism. I turned to the writings of patristic writers of the East and drank deeply from their well.

According to the desert fathers of the fourth century, we say no to certain thoughts and actions in order to say yes to the God who is beyond all thought and action. As one of the fathers said, "Just as it is impossible to see your face in troubled water, so also the soul, unless it is clear of alien thoughts, is not able to pray to God in contemplation."[9]

The *abbas* and *ammas* of the North African desert had left this world of compromise, adaptation, and lukewarm spirituality and had chosen solitude, silence, and prayer as the new way to be living witnesses to the crucified and risen Lord. They withdrew from the compulsive and manipulative actions of their power-hungry society to fight demons and encounter the God of love in the desert. By saying no to "normal" Christian society, they took up the cross of self-denial and asceticism and followed the radical call to leave father, mother, brother, and sister to go where God was leading. Thus they became the new martyrs, after the time of persecutions ceased, witnessing not with their blood but with their single-minded dedication to a humble life of manual work, fasting, and prayer.

The desert of self-denial and asceticism—the Egyptian desert of the *abbas* and *ammas,* but also our own spiritual desert—has a double quality: it is wilderness and paradise. It is wilderness, because in the desert we struggle against the "wild beasts" who attack us, the demons of boredom, sadness, anger, and pride. However, it is also paradise, because there we can meet God and taste already his peace and joy. Amma Syncletica said: "In the beginning, there is struggle and a lot of work for those who come near to God. But after that, there is indescribable joy. It is just like building a fire: at first it's smoky and your eyes water, but later you get the desired result. Thus we ought to light the divine fire in ourselves with tears and effort" (Desert Wisdom, pp. xii–xiii).

These fourth-century desert fathers and mothers became known for their wisdom, and it is easy to understand why many people from the cities and towns—laypeople, priests, and bishops—came to visit them and ask for advice, guidance, or just a word of comfort. It is also quite understandable that they themselves always considered it their primary obligation to be hospitable to their visitors and to help the poor and needy. Even the most severe form of asceticism was considered less important than service to a neighbor. That is why one of the wise men of the desert says, "Even if the brother who fasts six days were to hang himself by the nose, he could not equal the one who serves the sick."

Merton also bought the first volume of the works of John of the Cross to learn more about asceticism and contemplative prayer but had no idea where to begin reading: "These words I underlined, although they amazed and dazzled me with their import, were all too simple for me to understand. They were too naked, too stripped of all duplicity and compromise for my complexity, perverted by many appetites."[10] Nevertheless, he dug deeper and soon imposed upon himself a strongly ascetical lifestyle at Saint Bonaventure's College, where he taught before becoming a monk, as he began to understand that "dark night," the stripping away described by the 13th century Spanish mystic.

In reading the works of the nineteenth-century writer Saint Thérèse of Lisieux, he discovered that the requirements for saint-hood and contemplation were also present in normal civil society. One did not have to retreat to the desert to find God. Nor was spiritual depth reserved for some elite group. He wrote about her:

> The one thing that seemed to me more or less impos-
> sible was for grace to penetrate the thick, resilient hide of
> bourgeois smugness and really take hold of the immortal
> soul beneath that surface, in order to make something out
> of it. At best, I thought, such people might turn out to be
> harmless prigs: but great sanctity? Never! . . . However,
> no sooner had I got a faint glimpse of the real character
> and the real spirituality of St. Thérèse, than I was imme-
> diately and strongly attracted to her—an attraction that
> was the work of grace, since, as I say, it took me, in one

jump, clean through a thousand psychological obstacles and repugnancies.

Her "little way" of spirituality showed that a soul abandoned to the love of God that leads to a response of faithful deeds in everyday life can be one pleasing to God.

If Aldous Huxley introduced Merton to asceticism and Thérèse showed him the way of everyday spirituality, Ignatius of Loyola brought him all the way into contemplative prayer. The *Spiritual Exercises* had been standing in his bookcase for a long time, but he was a little bit afraid of them, because of "having somewhere acquired a false impression that if you did not look out they would plunge you head first into mysticism before you were aware of it." Still, he was attracted to prayer and contemplation and set up his own discipline:

As far as I remember, I devoted a whole month to the Exercises, taking one hour each day. I took a quiet hour, in the afternoon, in my room on Perry Street: and since I now lived in the back of the house, there were no street noises to worry me. It was really quite silent. With the windows closed, since it was winter, I could not even hear any of the neighborhood's five thousand radios.

The book said the room should be darkened, and I pulled down the blinds so that there was just enough light left for me to see the pages, and to look at the Crucifix on the wall over my bed. And the book also invited me to consider what kind of a position I should take for my meditation. It left me plenty of freedom of choice, so long as I remained more or less the way I was, once I had settled down, and did not go promenading around the room scratching my head and talking to myself.

So I thought and prayed awhile over this momentous problem, and finally decided to make my meditations sitting cross-legged on the floor. I think the Jesuits would have had a nasty shock if they had walked in and seen me doing their Spiritual Exercises sitting there like Mahatma Gandhi. But it worked very well. Most of the time I kept my eyes on the Crucifix or on the floor, when I did not have to look at the book.

And so, having prayed, sitting on the floor, I began to consider the reason why God had brought me into the world.[11]

LISTENING TO THE TEXTS

I learned much from Merton about the way the spiritual life unfolds in an individual's life, but there were differences that also illumined my own journey with God. We can be helped in discernment by reading the works of others, yet there is no single guidebook out there to discover. Unlike Thomas Merton, I did not have to come to the end of myself in order to be converted and baptized a Christian. I was born and baptized into a relationship with God through the Roman Catholic Church and felt from an early time a desire to be a priest. But my discovery, partially through Merton's writings, of the "pure nature of God" and of my very existence as being eternally held in the "memory of God" began to deepen through *spiritual reading*—as I opened my heart to the signs of God's presence and direction in the books and texts that called for my attention.

The ancient method of spiritual reading, whether listening to texts read out loud or in reflective reading by yourself, can be found in the instructions of Saint Augustine, Saint Bernard, Jean-Pierre de Caussade, and many others.[12] It is a time-tested way of listening for the movement of the Spirit in our lives. For example, in the fifth century, Saint Augustine advises his congregation to "listen to the Gospel as though the Lord himself were present. . . . The precious things that came from the mouth of the Lord were written down for us and kept for us and read aloud for us, and will be read by our children too, until the end of the world."[13]

In the twelfth century, Saint Bernard instructed his monks to read both sacred scripture and devotional books "from the heart" to devour their truth and preserve them in memory, in the same way you would eat bread to stay alive:

> For this is living bread and the food of the Spirit. While earthly bread is in the cupboard it can be stolen by a thief, gnawed by a mouse, or simply go bad from being kept too long. But if you eat it, what have you to fear? Keep the word of God in this way: for blessed are those who keep it. . . . Eat what is good and your soul will enjoy prosperity. Don't forget to eat your bread, lest your heart should dry up. If you keep the word of God like this, there is no doubt that it will keep you.[14]

Jean-Pierre de Caussade, in his eighteenth-century letters to those for whom he served as spiritual director, provides specific instructions on how to read a book spiritually:

> If you are to get from it all the good I anticipate, you must not throw yourself greedily upon it or let yourself be drawn on by curiosity as to what comes next. Fix your attention upon what you are reading without thinking about what follows. . . . Pause briefly, from time to time, to let these pleasant truths sink deeper and deeper into your soul, and allow the Holy Spirit time to work. . . . Simply let the truths sink into your heart rather than into your mind.[15]

Merton showed me how reading attentively gave him language to understand his core identity in the midst of the times in which he lived. Spiritual reading expanded his vision of God as the foundation of all life and deepened his understanding of the role of prayer and asceticism in spiritual growth. Throughout my life, I have continued to read the Bible and spiritual masters as well as biographies and volumes on current events. Spiritual reading and listening for the movement of the Spirit has helped me learn that God does speak through varied voices. And more importantly, God often reveals the contents of my own heart, as I slow and read not to know more but to be more fully known by God.

Exercises for Deeper Discernment

1. What books have shaped your life, your history with God? Write three paragraphs about the books or ideas that have shaped your "sacred history."

2. Thomas Merton's biography had a significant impact on Nouwen's view of God. Merton moved from seeing God as "grandfatherly" to the source and foundation of all life. What writers or texts have influenced your view of God? Where do you get the names and images you use when describing and addressing God? How might the name you use and your vision of God affect the way you understand God's guidance?

FOUR

Read the Book of Nature

While it is true that God is a hidden presence, we have only
to let nature speak to us about the God who is everywhere.
—*Henri Nouwen in "The Genesee Diary"*

Beyond books and people, nature also points to God and offers
signs and wonders indicating God's presence and will. The Book
of Nature, which cannot be reduced to words, reveals characteris-
tics of God and God's activity.[1] How do the sun and stars, plants
and animals, and natural rhythms speak of God's glory, wonder,
and ways? I must admit it has been easier for me to read words
on a page than to listen for God's revelation in the natural world
and events. Yet as I began to meet others who were more attuned
to God at work in the wonders of the world, I began to read the
gospels differently and see how my surroundings are also means
through which God can speak.

WALK WITH JESUS ON THE EARTH

As one who has spent my adult years as a priest, teacher, and writer, I haven't had to do much walking in my life. There have always been cars, planes, trains, and buses to take me from one place to another. My feet have not had much contact with dusty roads; there have always been wheels to make it easier for me to get from place to place without thinking much about the created world around me. But when I reread the gospels, paying attention to the way Jesus walked on the dust of the earth, I began to see that he felt the heat of the day and the cold of the night. He knew about the grass that withers and fades, the rocky soil, the thorny bushes, the barren trees, the flowers in the fields, and the rich harvest. He knew because he walked so much and felt in his own body both the harshness and the vitality of the seasons.

Jesus is deeply connected to the earth on which he walks. He observes the forces of nature, learns from them, teaches about them, and reveals that the God of Creation is the same God who sent him to give good news to the poor, sight to the blind, and freedom to the prisoners. He walks from village to village, sometimes alone and sometimes with others; as he walks, he meets the poor, the beggars, the blind, the sick, the mourners, and those who have lost hope. He listens attentively to those with whom he walks, and he speaks to them with the authority of a true companion on the road. He remains very close to the ground.

If I am to follow Jesus, then I, too, must remain close to the soil. Often I look up into the clouds and daydream about a better world. But my dreams will never bear fruit unless I keep turning my eyes again and again back to the dust of this earth and listening to what God is saying to me on the road of life. For I am connected to the earth and to all who walk the earth with me. Nature is not the background to our lives; it is a living gift that teaches us about the ways and will of the Creator. My friends who are more aware of the way nature teaches have shown me how to slow down and savor the way God's presence is woven into the natural world.

WALK WITH FRIENDS THROUGH THE WOODS

I remember a number of years ago taking a long walk with my friend Jutta through the forest of Compiegne in France when it was wet and foggy. No leaves dressed the trees, no sun rays beamed through the dark branches. But the forest revealed itself to us with new beauty: endless shades of gray and green, the mist quietly moving around the trunks of tall trees, hugging them gently. We stopped here and there just to gaze at the pathways and little trenches that vanished in the mist, leading perhaps to some mysterious place. Tall, straight trees everywhere spoke to us about peace, stability, harmony, rest, life and death, coming and going, staying and leaving. These great trees had been there long before we were born and will be there long after we are gone. But they, too, will fall down someday and merge with the soil from whence they came, to again nurture new shoots.

Suddenly we came to the edge of a valley where we could see far and wide. We saw the immense forest stretching out before us. As the fog moved in closer and surrounded us, it formed little clouds or columns of dense smoke. No birds could be heard, no deer seen, but the fog danced like a friendly spirit, keeping the trees company. The trees said good things, the spirits smiled, and we did not feel afraid or alone. This memory is not remarkable, but it is profound. Walking in the woods with my eyes and heart open offered a reminder that a walk with a friend can remind us of God's presence and peace even in the midst of confusing times. Just as fog is not uncommon in the natural world, perhaps confusion and lack of clarity are also part of living.

One of the people who helped me begin to see the wonder of the natural world is my good friend Robert Jonas, who is a committed environmentalist. On another trip to Europe, he and I spent a day in the Black Forest of Germany, in the tiny village of Horben, thirty minutes from Freiburg. It is beautifully situated in the midst of the pine-covered hills, and we felt transported to another world. Fields, trees, valleys and mountains, houses and barns were all made white by fresh snow. The bright sun made the white snow into an immaculate blanket decorated with countless glittering stars. As we walked through the fields, everything lay so still and quiet that we found ourselves whispering to each other, as if we didn't want to interrupt nature's silence. The quiet was as deep as any I could recall, and we entered into the splendor of creation. We felt grateful in our hearts and at one with our surroundings. The mystery of God's presence was all around. It was difficult to break the silence and continue on our way.

It is remarkable to see how prayer and contemplation open your eyes to nature, and how nature makes you more attentive to divine guidance. I once saw contemplation as something done best in the quiet of a monastery or behind a closed door. Now I know that nature can be a contemplative companion. Instead of trying to control and manipulate the circumstances of your life and the world around you, you become more receptive to God in the world. You no longer ignore or grab nature as if it were a thing to dominate or own, but rather caress it; you no longer examine but admire it. In return, nature reveals itself transformed and renewed—no longer an impediment to prayer but a means of discernment; instead of an invulnerable shield, a veil permitting a preview of unknown horizons.

Letting nature speak opens up new aspects of discerning the divine presence in what we so dimly see. What say the trees and stars? Sometimes we need to take a long walk through a forest, whether it be decorated with new growth and bright colors or in simple shades of gray, and ask God to reveal something of his ways, will, and character.

LET HEAVEN AND NATURE SING

When I began to awake to seeing nature as more than a metaphor—as a living revelation of God's ways—I looked back at how well taught I had been to experience God in nature, even if it took me time to fully grow into this way of seeking God. "The rain is a sign of God's blessing," said Abbot John Eudes in a talk on a special Sunday during the Eucharist at the Abbey of the Genesee, when I was there on retreat years ago. What he said about God in creation gave me a fuller sense of how God is always present.

"The Hebrew word for 'good' and 'blessing' at times means rain," Father John explained. "God is not far from us that we should have to descend to the depths of the sea or ascend to the clouds to find him. God's *presence* is in the things that are closest to us, things that we touch and feel, that we move and live with day by day. While it is true that God is a hidden presence, we have only to let nature speak to us about the God who is everywhere."

"When I walk into a garden," he continued, "I can embrace the present moment by pondering a single flower. The more beautiful and effervescent the flower, the more elusive and fragile is its life. Beauty by its very nature is fragile. Touch it too roughly and it's gone, grasp it too firmly and its petals fall away. It must be held onto lightly and gazed on attentively or it slips away. You cannot analyze it or pull it apart to see what it's made of or how it got there, if you want to experience the flower in the field. So, too, are our lives. Concrete yet so elusive. For who can fully analyze our lives or understand their many ways? But we can taste and feel them in the moment and refuse to pull them apart like the petals of a flower." Father John Eudes was expressing what Julian of Norwich and others knew: that "everything has being through the love of God." Be it a small flower or a hazelnut or any other created thing, something of God can be found in it.

GOD'S FIRST LANGUAGE IS NATURE

Dutch is my first language, yet I write often in English. It can be said that God's first language is nature, even if God is revealed through our ancient and enduring spiritual texts. You can read God's ways and will in the seasonal patterns and cycles of creation: life and death, planting and harvest, waiting for and basking in new life and resurrection. "Very truly, I tell you, unless a grain of wheat falls into the earth and dies, it remains just a single grain; but if it dies, it bears much fruit" (John 12:24).

Many of us who love books and the quest for spiritual knowledge have to be slowly tutored in the language of nature. Before joining the Trappists, Thomas Merton was too busy with his own inner life and journey to completely open to God in nature. Although he found it difficult to experience the joys of nature in the city, when he was with his friends at a summer cottage, nature began to speak, and he began to understand a language that he never found in books. His eyes wandered from the pages to the trees and on to the dark sky. In his autobiography he wrote:

> It was a cool summer evening. . . . With the book in my lap I looked down at the lights of the cars crawling up the road from the valley. I looked at the dark outline of the wooded hills and at the stars that were coming out in the eastern sky. The words of the Vulgate text rang and echoed in my heart: "Qui tacit Arcturum et Oriona . . ."; "Who makest Arcturus and Orion and Hyades and the inner parts of the South."[2]

Later, at the abbey, after living for many years in the Kentucky hills, Merton enjoyed an intimacy with nature that nourished his prayer life. This increasing ease with prayer had a deep effect on his life. Beyond his longing for a more disciplined lifestyle, there was a growing openness to the beauty of nature and freedom in respect to his environment. He became less intense, agitated, needy, and restless. In the natural environment in which he lived—which he had hardly noticed earlier—opened up for him a magnificent and transformed beauty and a richer view of God's world:

When I look at your heavens, the work of your fingers,
the moon and the stars that you have established;
what are human beings that you are mindful of them,
mortals that you care for them. . . .
O Lord, our Sovereign,
how majestic is your name in all the earth! (Ps. 8:3, 4, 9)

When we relate to the trees, the rivers, the mountains, the fields, and the oceans as objects that we can use according to our real or fabricated needs, nature is opaque and does not reveal to us its true being. When a tree is nothing but a potential chair, it ceases to tell us much about growth; when a river is only a dumping place for industrial wastes, it can no longer speak to us about movement; and when a flower is nothing more than a model for a plastic decoration, it has little to say about the simple beauty of life.

Our difficult and now urgent task is to realize that nature is not a possession to be conquered but a gift to be received with respect and gratitude. Only when we make a deep bow to the rivers, oceans, hills, and mountains that offer us a home—only then can they become transparent and reveal to us their real meaning. All of nature conceals great secrets that cannot be revealed if we do not listen carefully and patiently to God's hidden language.

Nature desires for us to discern the great story of God's love to which it points. The plants and animals with whom we live teach us about birth, growth, maturation, and death, about the need for gentle care, and especially about the importance of patience and hope. And even more profoundly, the properties of water, oil, bread, and wine all point beyond themselves to the great story of our re-creation. Food and drink, mountains and rivers, oceans and skies—all become transparent when nature discloses itself to those with eyes to see and ears to hear what the Great Spirit of God is saying to us.

THE CALL TO RENEW CREATION

Over time I began to understand that all creation belongs and rests in the arms of its Creator; and that the one who would commune with God by eating and drinking at the table must first hear and celebrate the voices of nature, translating for the benefit of others.

When we think of the oceans and mountains, forests and deserts, trees, plants and animals, the sun, the moon, the stars, and all the galaxies as God's creation, waiting eagerly for their renewal (Rom. 8:20–21), we can only stand in awe of God's majesty and all-embracing plan of redemption. It is not just we human beings who wait for our salvation in the midst of our suffering: all creation groans and moans with us, longing to reach its full freedom.

In this way, we are indeed brothers and sisters not only of all other men and women in the world but also of all that surrounds us. Yes, we have to love and respect the fields full of wheat, the snowcapped mountains, the roaring seas, the wild and tame animals, the huge redwoods, and the little daisies. Everything in creation belongs, with us, to the large family of God.

How expansive is the vision of what God is doing in my life and yours when we can embrace the full reality that our final calling and homecoming involves not just ourselves and our fellow human beings but all of creation. The full freedom of the children of God is to be shared by the whole earth, and our complete renewal in the resurrection includes the renewal of the universe. This is the great vision of God's redeeming work through Christ. This is Isaiah's vision of the Peaceable Kingdom—"The wolf and the lamb shall feed together, the lion shall eat straw like the ox; . . . They shall not hurt or destroy on all my holy mountain, says the Lord" (Isa. 65:25 NRSV)—and we must try to keep this vision alive. True discernment will engage us in the great call of God in which we participate. It is not enough for me to discern God's will for my life. I must discern God's desires for my life as one small but important part of God's great call to renew and redeem all the earth.

This is why the saints and prophets through the ages, seeking life's hidden meaning, have tried to live as close to nature as possible. Saint Benedict moved his community to the top of Mount Cassino in the sixth century; Saint Francis considered the elements to be Brother Sun and Sister Moon and the animals as part of his extended family in the twelfth century; Saint Bruno retreated to the craggy Alps in the eleventh century; but also Thomas Merton, who lived in the woods of Kentucky, and the Benedictine monks, who continue to build their monasteries in our own time in places like an isolated canyon in New Mexico. Still today, many young people leave the cities and go out into the country to find peace by listening to the voices of nature. And nature does indeed speak: the birds to Saint Francis, the trees to the Native Americans, the river to Siddhartha, the stars to Merton. The closer we come to nature, the more we touch the spirit of life.

We who have been nurtured by Western Christianity have much to learn from Native Americans about how to hear the voices of the rivers, the trees, the birds, and the flowers, which are constantly telling us about our own condition of life, our beauty, and our mortality. A Wintu Indian once said:

The white people never cared for land or deer or bear. When we Indians kill meat, we eat it all up. When we dig roots, we make little holes. . . . We shake down acorns and pine nuts. We don't chop down trees. We only use dead wood. But the white people plow up the ground, pull up the trees, kill everything. The tree says, "Don't, I am sore. Don't hurt me." But they chop it down and cut it up. The spirit of the land hates them. . . . The Indians never hurt anything, but the white people destroy all.[3]

Native Americans feel that they are part of nature, brothers and sisters to all creatures. They make their artwork in obedience to nature. In their masks human and animal faces merge; in their pottery they use vegetables, such as the gourd, for models. It is nature that teaches them the forms they can make with their own hands. The earth is God's body, and they know how to listen to what God's body has to teach.

Once we become sensitive to the voices of nature, we may hear sounds from a world where humanity and nature both find their form. Once we become more aware of the voices of all that surround us, growing in respect and reverence for the God of all creation, we will also be able to truly care for all creatures, who are embedded in nature like a sapphire in a golden ring.

Dear Lord, you are the Word of God through whom all creation came into being: rivers and trees, mountains and valleys, birds and horses, wheat and corn, sun and stars, rain and thunder, wind and storm, and above all, people—male and female, young and old, black and white, brown and red, farmers and teachers, monks and businessmen. You, O Lord, can be found in all your creation. I thank you for the beauty of all that is.[4]

EXERCISES FOR DEEPER DISCERNMENT

1. Walk with Jesus on the earth. Drive down a dirt road, get out of the car, and walk on the dust of the earth as Jesus did. Pick one of the parables found in Mark 4. Read it outside and listen to what God might be saying through both the Book of the Bible and the Book of Nature. Reflect on how you discern differently when you "read" these two books together.

2. Walk with friends through the woods. Find a trail and set out on a journey in search of beauty. Instead of having a conversation, withhold your words and keep silent. Observe and be present to what you see and hear. Drink deeply from the well of creation. "Taste and see that the Lord is good."

3. Listen to heaven and nature sing. Alone or with friends, get close to nature. Read Isaiah 55:12 out loud: For you shall go out in joy and be led forth in peace; the mountains and the hills before you shall break forth into singing, and all the trees of the field shall clap their hands. As you listen to the music of nature, can you discern the singing of the trees? What would it mean for you to clap with the trees or dance with the mountains? Does this kind of engagement with nature come naturally to you or does it feel forced? Reflect on your relationship with the created world. Do you see the sun and stars as your brothers and sisters? Do you see yourself as a part of God's work to redeem the whole of creation? What might God be showing you about your place and purpose in his great purposes? Does this wide-angle view add perspective to your quest to discern what God is up to in your life?

FIVE

Pay Attention to People in Your Path

God speaks to us through the people
who speak to us about the things of God.
—*Henri Nouwen*

While it is true that God reveals wisdom and direction through
the Bible and the books and articles we read, as well as the Book
of Nature, it also is true that God speaks through the people
we meet in daily life. When I joined L'Arche Daybreak, where
people with disabilities are at the center of the community, no
one cared that I write books or give lectures to university audiences and church groups around the world. My achievements
did not impress them. What they cared deeply about was how
consistently I showed up for them and showed them how much I
loved them.

In the everyday routines and conversations of life, I began to hear the voice of God anew. The Spirit of God seemed to speak directly to them and through them, unmediated by books or intellectual discussion. Some members of my community may not have a lot of physical or mental capacities and skills, but in their poverty and simplicity they are more open to God than I am. Because, their center of being is wide open to God, they seem to be able to see and speak directly to the heart of my concerns. "Henri, do you love me? Will you be home tonight? Will you take me with you? Will you care for me?" They helped me see that I could write about being God's beloved, but it was in my relationships with them that I would learn what it meant to be loved and to give love as part of learning what it means to love God, myself, and my neighbor as Jesus commanded.

People we meet, some great in the eyes of the world and some almost invisible to the larger society, are often conduits of God's wisdom. When I met Mother Teresa during a visit to Rome, I *saw* immediately that her inner attention was focused only on Jesus, and through him she came to see the poorest of the poor, to whom she dedicated her life. When ordinary social, psychological, or medical questions were brought to her, she did not answer them on the level they were raised. Instead, she addressed them with a divine logic and from a spiritual place and perspective that remains unfamiliar to most of us. That is why many found her ways simplistic, naive, and out of touch. Like Jesus, she challenged her listeners to move with her to that place where things can be seen as God sees them and to look beyond the surface to the place of divine encounter or call.

In my case, I had asked her for advice on what to do about my spiritual distractions and temptations. After she listened to my unique complications and elaborate explanations of the trials of my life, she burst my bubble by saying simply, "Well, when you spend one hour a day adoring your Lord and never do anything which you know to be wrong . . . you will be fine!"

Her response startled me. I had expected her to diagnose and discuss my very pressing questions, but I suddenly realized that I had asked questions "from below" and she had given an answer "from above," pointing me in the direction of divine presence. She knew that even if I better understood my distractions and problems, something else remained: a call to live closer to the heart of God. At first her answer didn't seem to fit my questions, but then I began to see that her answer came from God's place of healing and not from the place of my complaints. Getting answers to my questions is not the goal of the spiritual life. Living in the presence of God is the greater call. The gift of discernment is the ability to hear and see from God's perspective and to offer that wisdom from above to others. Truly, God spoke to me through the mouth of Mother Teresa. She called me back to the discipline of prayer and being in God's presence, which is the starting and ending place out of which guidance emerges.

Someone who showed me how important it is to learn to listen not just to people like Mother Teresa, whom many people revere, but to attend to the voices of the people we live with most intimately was Father Thomas Philippe. Père Thomas is a Dominican priest who cofounded the L'Arche community with Jean Vanier in Trosly, France, in the mid-1960s. Even though he has died, he is still considered the community's spiritual father. He believed that God speaks primarily through family members and close friends with whom we have a primary relationship. We spent many hours talking about the way an intimate and intensive relationship with one's spouse, parents, child, or friend creates a dynamic interpersonal relation that also is transpersonal and spiritual, and thus can become a vehicle for divine presence and direction, though in a limited way. For many who come to L'Arche, primary relationships have been severed or strained due to the difficulties of living with disabilities. One of the most healing aspects of L'Arche is the way the members of the community—those who are able-bodied and those who are not, those who can speak and those who can't—are all seen as mediators of love and grace by those in the community.

I met Père Thomas at L'Arche in 1985, when he was eighty years old and fully active as a priest in the community. Because of his extraordinary gifts of discernment and wisdom, some called him the "John of the Cross of our time." He thoroughly understood the way God speaks through imperfection. It was a profound experience for me to be in the presence of someone whose French I could hardly understand but who nevertheless communicated deeply and convincingly the mystery of God's presence in the people among us.

Like Mother Teresa, he asked questions that pushed beyond the surface problems many of us focus on. For example, when we discussed how our parents wounded us and how God was the only true parent, he asked, "Why can we not think of our biological parents as created beings who refract for us some of the divine fatherhood and motherhood, instead of God as a creation of our minds which compensates for our parents' imperfection?" Such profound questions about the existence and nature of God do not belong to the field of psychology alone, as they inquire into the very nature of how God is incarnate and present in real flesh-and-blood people. Père Thomas had a theological understanding of the trusting heart—that all human expressions of love which come to us in life, though limited and imperfect, are in fact manifestations of the unlimited and perfect love of God. "Somehow," he said, "even as small children, we are in touch with a love greater, deeper, and stronger than our parents or teachers can offer us."

As a theologian, he considered all human relationships to be "signs which point to the inner life of God." Our three primary sets of relationships are usually with the parents who raised us, close friends whom we consider peers, and immediate family with whom we live (spouse or community). These primary relationships reflect our relationship (or lack of a felt relationship) with God as Father/Creator, Son/Redeemer, and Spirit/ Sustainer. These relationships, for better or worse, can lead us to a more intimate communion with the triune God. At first, this might sound idealistic. But once we are willing to see human persons as living signs and all of life as the continuing manifestation of God's love, we can begin to *see through* the relationships in our life as gifts of God that help mold and shape us, reminding us of the inner quality of God's own love.

Even if our mother or father or brother or sister or spouse or friend couldn't love us in every way we might have liked, Père Thomas began to show me that each one did reflect an aspect of God's love, and when taken together they reflected the fullness of God in a way I had often missed in focusing on what each one was not able to offer.

In this conviction, Thomas Philippe was in essential agreement with Thomas Merton—who also wrote significantly about the need to pay attention to the people God puts in your path if you want to discern what God is up to in your life.

LIVING SIGNPOSTS: PEOPLE WHO HELPED POINT MERTON TO GOD

Merton's *Secular Journal* and *The Seven Storey Mountain* are full of names of people he knew in his youth. Next to books, it was people who became living signs pointing Merton to God and toward making his home at Gethsemani Abbey. Three names in particular stand out as major shaping influences and luminous figures: Daniel Walsh, Dr. Bramachari, and Bob Lax. When I read Merton's autobiography, I began to see how teachers and friends spoke the truth of God into Merton's life in ways books never could.

Daniel Walsh, a guest lecturer at Columbia University, introduced Merton to Thomas Aquinas (1225–1274) and Duns

Scotus (1266–1308), two of the great theologian-philosophers of the late Middle Ages. These philosophers and their respective ideas of God as the "primary mover" and the "infinite being" inspired his imagination and imposed some order on his myriad ideas and feelings. Walsh, he said, "had nothing of the supercilious self-assurance of the ordinary professor: he did not need this frail and artificial armor for his own insufficiency. He did not need to hide behind tricks and vanities; he never even needed to be brilliant. In his smiling simplicity he used to efface himself entirely in the solid and powerful mind of St. Thomas."[1]

Even before Merton began to attend Walsh's lectures, he had visited him and presented him with his idea of becoming a priest. Together they talked about all the different orders and eventually settled on the Franciscans as the best type for Merton. But then Walsh told him enthusiastically about Gethsemani and urged him to go there on retreat. This conversation would lead Merton to discern his calling to join the Trappists. Years later, Walsh came to Gethsemani to teach philosophy, and in 1967 he himself was ordained a priest in the diocese of Louisville. The teacher and student roles helped each discern their vocation as they learned together.

A completely different figure who left a deep influence on Thomas Merton was the Indian monk referred to as Dr. Bramachari (which is the Hindu term for monk). Merton wrote about him with much humor, great respect, and deep reverence. When he met Bramachari for the first time, at Grand Central Station in New York, he wrote: "There stood a shy little man, very happy, with a huge smile, all teeth, in the midst of his brown face. And on the top of his head was a yellow turban with Hindu prayers written all over it in red. And, on his feet, sure enough: sneakers."

Merton and Bramachari soon became friends. Merton admired the sympathetic way in which Bramachari criticized the Western world and relativized everything that others in the university world found so important:

He was never sarcastic, never ironical or unkind in his criticisms: in fact he did not make many judgments at all, especially adverse ones. He would simply make statements of fact, and then burst out laughing—his laughter was quiet and ingenuous, and it expressed his complete amazement at the very possibility that people should live the way he saw them living all around him.[2]

Bramachari did not at all try to give Merton insight into his own beliefs, let alone force any convictions on him. On the contrary, he said to Merton, "There are many beautiful mystical books written by the Christians. You should read St. Augustine's *Confessions* and *The Imitation of Christ*." Thus he was all the more impressed when this Hindu monk pointed him to the Christian mystical tradition. Later he wrote: "Now that I look back on those days, it seems to me very probable that one of the reasons why God had brought him all the way from India, was that he might say just that." Ironically, this Hindu monk helped guide Merton's youthful curiosity about the East and made him sensitive to the richness of the Western Christian mystical tradition. How like God to speak through an unexpected source in a surprising way.

Of all the people who played a role in Merton's journey to Gethsemani, Bob Lax is certainly the most fascinating and perhaps also the central figure. The name Bob Lax appears often in *The Seven Storey Mountain*, and this remarkable figure emerges time and again at critical moments. He was not a teacher like Walsh, nor was he as interesting an outsider as Bramachari. Lax belonged to the small circle of literary friends with whom Merton spent his student years in New York City. He was an intimate friend indeed, but described with so much admiration and sympathy that it is clear how Merton constantly fell under his spell.

Merton saw Lax for the first time sitting in the midst of a group of editors at the student magazine *Jester*, and later tried to describe him:

He was a kind of combination of Hamlet and Elias. A potential prophet, but without rage. A king, but a Jew too. A mind full of tremendous and subtle intuitions, and every day he found less and less to say about them, and resigned himself to being inarticulate. In his hesitations, though without embarrassment or nervousness at all, he would often curl his long legs all around a chair, in seven different ways, while he was trying to find a word with which to begin. He talked best sitting on the floor.

And the secret of his constant solidity I think has always been a kind of natural, instinctive spirituality, a kind of inborn direction to the living God. Lax has always been afraid he was in a blind alley, and half aware that, after all, it might not be a blind alley, but God, infinity.

He had a mind naturally disposed, from the very cradle, to a kind of affinity for Job and St. John of the Cross. And I now know that he was born so much of a contemplative that he will probably never be able to find out how much.

To sum it up, even the people who have always thought he was "too impractical" have always tended to venerate him—in the way people who value material security unconsciously venerate people who do not fear insecurity.[3]

Lax in many ways was a prophet and guide for Merton. There was tremendous simplicity and power in their relationship. Of all the people Merton knew in his youth, Lax was undoubtedly the one closest to him. Lax was his best friend, but he never used him to avoid his call to solitude. Rather, he describes him as one of the many signs on his way to God. The power of friendship is great if it doesn't find all its meaning in itself. If people expect too much from each other, they can do each other harm; disappointment and bitterness can overpower love and even replace it. But in the practice of discernment in daily life, we can learn to appreciate our closest friends, family members, and sometimes complete strangers, as signposts pointing toward God. Friends may be guides who see what we may not be able to see ourselves.

LIVING SIGNS WHO HELPED ME FIND A HOME

For me, some of the critical people in my life who helped me follow a call to L'Arche were Robert Jonas, Nathan Ball, and Sue Mosteller. Unique among my many, many dear friends from different seasons of my life, these three intersected my path at critical points and helped me hear the inner voice of love.[4] Here, I will reflect on the ways each pointed me toward God.

Robert Jonas: The Gift of Spiritual Friendship
My decision to leave Harvard Divinity School was a difficult one. Over many months of tearful prayers and sleepless nights, I tried to distinguish the many voices in my head. Would I be following or betraying my vocation by leaving? The outer voices kept saying, "You can do so much good here. People need you!" The inner voices kept saying, "What good is it to preach the gospel to others while losing your own soul?" Discernment of spirits was required, and my dear friend and former student, Robert Jonas, became for me a spiritual companion and guide at a critical time of personal confusion and exploration.

It took over a year for me to be willing to explore a new possible vocation and home among people with physical and intellectual disabilities. Finally, through discussions with Jonas, I discerned that my increasing inner darkness, my feelings of rejection, my inordinate need for affirmation and affection, and my deep sense of not belonging were clear signs that I needed to go.

The deep connection I felt with Jean Vanier and his L'Arche community in France made it easier to leave Harvard and go to Trosly-Breuil in 1985 for a year of prayer and discernment. L'Arche proved to be a wonderful place not only to recover from terminal academia but to explore a new calling. When Madame Vanier, Jean's eighty-seven-year-old mother, threw her arms around me as I stepped into her house at L'Arche, it felt like coming home.

That very day, I heard something like an inner urging to start keeping a journal again. After my trip to Latin America four years earlier, I had given up daily writing. But it suddenly dawned on me that if this year were going to be a year of prayer, reading, writing, and recovery, while listening carefully to the inner movements of the Spirit, then how better to get in touch with God's work in me than by recording what was happening to me day after day? If this were really going to be a year of discernment, an honest journal might help me as much now as it had in the past.

Less than a month passed in France before I began to miss my friends in Boston. On September 10, I wrote in my journal: "A very hard day. I had been waiting for my dear friend Jonas, who took me to the airport in Boston and promised to come and visit me in France. . . . I had the impression that he was eager to see me and that he would find a way. When I called him, he explained that his plans had changed, and that he had to delay his visit. . . . I felt deeply hurt."

In coping with those familiar feelings of rejection, I told myself, "Henri, if you really want to be less visible in the world, less known and more forgotten, then try to take this experience and use it to become more grateful and more spiritual. Trust that hiddenness will give you new eyes to see yourself, your world, and your God. People cannot give you new eyes—only the one who loves you without limits."

My journal recorded what I knew I should do and wanted to do on some level, but my actions were slow to follow during that first month in France. I prayed for a few quiet moments, asking Jesus to help me, and tried to do my work as best I could. "Lord, give me the peace and joy that only you can give."

Two weeks later, Jonas called again from Cambridge to say, "I want to come visit you in October!" Once we discussed specific dates and places, I let go of my resentment and felt again his caring and faithful friendship.

Jonas came and stayed with me at L'Arche for ten days, visiting community members, attending workshops, meeting specialists, and seeing the surrounding areas with me. It felt to me like showing a foreigner my hometown and discovering it myself in the process. As a psychologist, Jonas was the kind of friend who raised questions, noticed events, and made comparisons differently from me, and he helped me uncover a different L'Arche from what I had seen so far.

During our time together, we were able to talk about our expectations in this spiritual friendship. It was hard for me to speak of my feelings of being rejected or imposed upon, of my desire for affirmation as well as my need for space, of insecurity and mistrust, of fear and love. But as I entered into these feelings, I also discovered the real problem—expecting from a friend what only Christ can give.

Jonas challenged me to move out of the center and stop acting as if my life were the only one affected by true friendship. He, too, had a life; he, too, had his struggles; he, too, had unfulfilled needs and imperfections. As I tried to understand his life, I felt deep compassion for him. I no longer felt the need to judge him for not paying enough attention to me. I learned that once you can see another concretely, recognizing the similar struggles and unfilled needs, you can step back a bit from your own life and understand that, in true friendship, there is give and take as two people learn to dance.

I also learned afresh that friendship requires a constant willingness to forgive each other for not being Christ, and a willingness to ask Christ himself to be the true center of the relationship. When Christ does not mediate a friendship, that relationship easily becomes demanding, manipulating, and oppressive, and fails to offer the other the space to grow. True friendship requires closeness, affection, support, and mutual encouragement, but also distance, space to grow, freedom to be different, and solitude. To nurture both aspects of a relationship, we must experience a deeper and more lasting affirmation than any human relationship can offer.

As I struggled to understand my need for close friendships, I came to understand why Jesus sent out his disciples into the world in groups of two. Together, they could maintain the spirit of peace and love and the affirmation they found in his company, and they could share these gifts with everyone they met.

Nathan Ball: The Invitation to Become a Brother
One of the community members I met that year at L'Arche was Nathan Ball, with whom I gradually became close friends. To this day I consider him closer than a brother. I have always considered spiritual friendship to be one of the greatest gifts God has given me. It is the most life-giving gift I can imagine. I met many wonderful, loving, caring people at L'Arche Trosly— together a source of great joy to me—and I remember each one with gratitude and fondness. Yet, of the many, there was something quite special about my friendship with Nathan. He was a wonderful listener who was wise and faithful about the ways of God. I felt deeply that he would become a new companion in life, a new presence that would last wherever I went.

Nathan is a Canadian who was raised a Baptist but entered the Roman Catholic Church just before coming to L'Arche to live and work as an assistant. When I first saw him with his friends in the foyer outside the chapel, I was deeply moved by his compassion and the generous affection he showed to those who were poor and broken. It was the fruit of caring for a brother with a physical disability who had died.

I was not aware of how significant our relationship had become until he left for a month to visit family and friends in Canada. I missed his presence greatly. As we talked about our future plans, it became clear that God had brought us together for a reason. Nathan planned to begin theological studies in Toronto the following fall and to live at Daybreak—a L'Arche affiliate community nearby. And I was being called to move to Daybreak as the resident priest in the community. I could not help but feel that his friendship would make it easier to follow that call.

In December 1985, I received a long letter from Daybreak, Canada, formally inviting me to join their community near Toronto. It was the first time in my life that I had been explicitly *called* to a new ministry. All my work as a priest since my ordination had been the result of my own initiative. I myself chose my work at the Menninger Clinic, Notre Dame, Yale, Harvard, and in Latin America. My bishops in the Netherlands had always agreed with and supported the choices I made. Now a faith community was saying, "We call you to live with us; to give to us and receive from us." I knew that the invitation was not a job offer but rather a genuine call to live with the poor. They had no money to offer, no attractive living quarters, no prestige. This was a wonderful and compelling new thing: a concrete call to follow Christ, to leave the world of success, accomplishment, and honor, and to trust Jesus and him alone. So often I had prayed, "Lord, show me your will and I will do it." If I ever wanted a concrete sign of Jesus's will for me, this was it. I felt within me that something was coming to a conclusion and something new was beginning. My academic period was ending, and I was being asked to move in a new direction.

At the end of August 1986, I left France and arrived at Daybreak, the L'Arche community in Canada, and moved into the New House with six residents with disabilities—Rose, Adam, Bill, John, Trevor, and Raymond. They and their assistants welcomed me warmly to my new home and role as pastor. As I settled into my new vocation and community, I came to think of my friendship with Nathan as a safe place in the midst of all the transitions and changes. "Whatever happens," I said to myself, "at least I have a friend to rely on, to go to for support, to be consoled by in hard moments." But somehow along the way, I had made Nathan the center of my emotional stability. My old needs and desire for attention and affirmation surfaced again. My new dependency and insecurity prevented me from making Christ and the community the true center of my life.

The Daybreak community gradually became my home, but it was not without great cost. At a certain point, Nathan said he could no longer be friends with me because of my possessiveness and dependency. Our friendship broke, which made life confusing and complicated as we lived in this small community together. I slipped into a depression that caused me to leave the community for several months. I have told my story of despair and recovery elsewhere,[5] but what I want to say here is that my relationship with Nathan was wonderfully restored and healed. It took three years of intentional spiritual work, strength, courage, fidelity, acceptance of counseling, and community support for that miracle of reconciliation to occur in our community. I reached a healthy place in which I was able to stop projecting my needs on another human being. We both came to understand that each of us is limited in our capacity to be for another what is needed, and learned to forgive each other for not being God. In this way, Nathan and I were free to be true friends and brothers. The restoration was God's sign to me to claim my own belovedness and come home. I learned that people can be signs and helpful companions, but only God can guide and fully heal the wounded places in each of us.

Sue Mosteller: *The Opportunity to Become the Father Figure*
It was during that long period of immense inner pain and feelings of rejection that another friend spoke a word of hope I desperately needed to hear, opening up a new phase of growth on my journey home. When I left the community to work directly

on my inner healing, I took with me only a few books and small reproductions of my favorite pieces of art. I took a reproduction of Rembrandt's painting of the parable of the prodigal son, and I found some consolation in reading about the tormented life of the great Dutch painter and in learning about the difficult journey that ultimately enabled him to paint this magnificent work. The beauty and pain of his life were profoundly painted into his works.

Sue Mosteller, a sister of the Community of Saint Joseph who had been with the Daybreak community since the early seventies and had played an important role in bringing me there, had given me indispensable support when things became difficult. She had encouraged me to struggle through whatever needed to be fulfilled to reach true inner freedom. She would not let me blame anyone else or think there was some easy way to regain my sense of inner belovedness.

When she visited me in my "hermitage," she not only reminded me of how much I was loved and missed but delivered a strong message that I really needed to hear. She spoke about the prodigal son parable and painting that meant so much to me, and she said, "Whether you are the younger son or the older son, you have to realize that you are called to become the father. That's who we need you to be at Daybreak."

Her words struck me like a thunderbolt because, after all my years of living with the painting and looking at the old man cradling his son, it had never occurred to me that the father, the one who welcomed others home, was the one who expressed most fully my vocation in life.

Sue did not give me much chance to protest but continued to speak God's truth right into me: "You have been looking for friends all your life; you have been craving affection as long as I've known you; you have been interested in thousands of things; you have been begging for attention, appreciation, and affirmation left and right. The time has come to claim your true vocation—to be a father who can welcome his children home."

She continued saying what God needed to say to me: "We at Daybreak and most people around you don't need you to be a good friend or even a kind brother. We need you to be a father figure who can claim for himself the authority of true compassion. Look at the father in your painting, and you will know who you are called to be."[6]

I looked again at the hands of the father in Rembrandt's painting and saw the two hands, one of a man and the other of a woman. The artist painted the female hand from an earlier painting of the Jewish bride—delicate, gentle, tender, protecting, and caring. The male hand is Rembrandt's own hand. It expresses who he is as father, supporter, defender, and giver of freedom. Both are hands of love, holding and letting go. I remembered Jean Vanier speaking about hands. He described the hands that gently encircle a wounded bird as being also open to allow movement and freedom to fly. Jean believes that each of us needs to have both hands around us. One says, "I've got you and I hold you safe because I love you and I'll never be apart from you. Don't be afraid." The other says, "Go, my child, find your way, make mistakes, learn, suffer, grow, and become whom you need to be. Don't be afraid. You are free and I am always near." These are the hands of unconditional love.

Besides Jonas, Nathan, and Sue, who were close to me at critical points, I have in my life many close friends and neighbors, community members and mentors, who are living signs of God's love and direction in good times and bad.[7] Beyond family and friends, I also feel a special closeness to certain "saints" in the church's memory who speak to me of faithful witness and strength and sometimes provide guidance in time of need. Together, God's people ground me in the reality and wholeness of Christ and his church, holding me firm and safe in God's loving embrace. God speaks regularly to us through people who talk to us about the things of God. Certain people become living signs that point us to God. Whether in life or in memory, the people God puts in our lives can help guide us and show us the way.

EXERCISES FOR DEEPER DISCERNMENT

1. Think back over the past week or month and review the words others have said that remain in your memory. We all have phrases, observations, or compliments others have spoken that stay with us. Write these down and see if they tell you something about this time in your life. In conversations with friends like Jonas, Nathan, and Sue, Nouwen identified his inner darkness, feelings of rejection, inordinate need for affirmation and affection, and deep sense of not belonging as clear signs that he needed to make a change. What you recall from conversations in your own life need not be as emotionally charged as Nouwen's to help you discern how you are being called right now.

2. Identify three people in your life with whom you share your questions and doubts. See if you can describe what each offers you. For Nouwen, Jonas brought psychological insight and a call to see empathy as key to mutual friendship; Nathan brought deep peace and theological insight; and Sue brought a prophetic call to live through his pain to become a compassionate father figure for others. What do the three people in your life reflect back to you? It might be fruitful to ask each one to spend a couple of hours in conversation and lovingly share their gifts of friendship with you. Pay attention to what each one says, for they might offer signs to help you along your path.

3. When Henri's friendship with Nathan broke, he had to learn to forgive him for not being God or fulfilling all his needs, so he could accept the great gifts he could offer without imposing impossible demands that could not be met by any other human being. Is there anyone you need to forgive and reconcile with so that you can again offer the great gift of friendship to each other?

SIX

Discern the Signs of the Times

Certain events—current events, historical events, critical incidents and life circumstances—serve as signposts pointing to the will of God and the new creation for those with eyes to see and ears to hear.

—*Henri Nouwen*

Frequently the news features people who declare that we are living in the end of times. Fear and worry can affect our interpretation of the events we see or hear about. I do believe that we are living in the end of times, but I take that to mean that we are living under God's promise that "all things are being made new." For me, living in the end of times does not mean that creation will soon come to an end, but it does mean that all the signs of the end that Jesus mentions are already with us: wars and revolutions, conflicts between nations, earthquakes, plagues, famines, and persecutions (see Luke 21:9–12). Jesus describes the events of our world as announcements that this world is not our final dwelling place and that the "Son of Man" will come to bring us our full freedom. "Now when these things begin to take place," Jesus says, "stand up and raise your heads, because your redemption is drawing near" (Luke 21:28 NRSV). How, then, do we begin to discern what the events of our times reveal about God's good purposes for us and for all of creation?

GOD'S TIME IS TIMELESS

Thomas Merton identified the "signs of the times" as *kairos*—a quality of time that is eternal, when time is full of meaning and events point to divine purpose. In one of many reflections on the topic, he wrote, "The Bible is concerned with time's fullness, the time for an event to happen, the time for an emotion to be felt, the time for a harvest or for the celebration of a harvest."[1] The Bible can be a good guide for our interpretation of events as we look to discern what God is doing and remember that God's design and final purpose is that God will ultimately reign and God's ways of love will prevail. God's ways are not always our ways. God's timetable is not always our timetable. Discernment calls us to settle into God's ways of measuring time.

Clock time (*chronos*) is divided into minutes, hours, days, and weeks, and its compartments dominate our lives. In chronological time, what happens to us is a series of disconnected incidents and accidents that we seek to manage or subdue to feel in control of our lives. Time becomes a burden unless we convert it into God's time.

God's time (*kairos*) has to do with opportunity and fullness of meaning, moments that are ripe for their intended purpose. When we see time in light of our faith in the God of history, we see that the events of this year are not just a series of happy or unhappy events but part of the shaping hands of God, who wants to mold our world and our lives. Even when life seems harried and continues to have hard moments, we can believe that something good is happening amid all of this. We get glimpses of how God might be working out his purposes in our days. Time becomes not just something to get through or manipulate or manage, but the arena of God's good work in us. Whatever happens—good things or bad, pleasant or problematic—we ask, "What might God be doing here?" We see the events of the day as continuing occasions to change the heart. Time points beyond itself and begins to speak to us of God.

God's time is timeless. Kairos contains both past and future events in the present moment. Words like *after* and *before,* or *first* or *last,* belong to mortal life and chronology. God is all in all, the beginning and end of time, and the deeper meaning of history. To gain this wider perspective, we first look backward to see how the seemingly unrelated events of our lives have brought us to where we are now. Like the people of Israel, who repeatedly reflected on their history and discovered God's guiding hand in the many painful events that led them to Jerusalem, so we pause to discern God's presence in the events that have made or unmade us. For by not remembering, we allow forgotten memories to intrude into the present and become independent forces with crippling effects on our lives. Forgetting the past is like turning our most intimate teacher against us. Remembering the past in this way allows us to live in the present and gain hope for the future, until *chronos* is converted to *kairos.*

This view of time helps us practice patience in discernment. If we are patient, we can look at all the events of each day—expected and unexpected—as holding promise for us. Patience is the attitude that says we cannot force life but have to let it grow in its own time. Patience lets us see the people we meet, the events of the day, and the unfolding history of our times as all part of that slow process of development and final liberation.

Given the nature of *kairos,* let's take a look at how certain *events*—critical events, current events, historical events, and even life circumstances—can serve as signposts pointing to the will of God and the new creation for those with eyes to see and ears to hear.

CRITICAL EVENTS CAN REVEAL DIVINE PURPOSE

Life is God's initiative and can end or change suddenly, unexpectedly, and unpredictably. When we humans are ready to give up hope and resign ourselves to inevitability, God intervenes and reveals completely new beginnings. The resurrection of Jesus is God's sign breaking through every form of human fatalism and despair. In every critical event, there is an opportunity for God to act creatively and reveal a deeper truth than what we see on the surface of things. God also can turn around critical incidents and seemingly hopeless situations in our lives and reveal light in darkness.

For example, almost a year before making L'Arche Daybreak my home, I visited the community for several days. I had a chance to meet all the assistants and community members, and celebrated the Eucharist with some of them. While I was there, Raymond, one of the core community members, was hit by a car while crossing a busy street and thrown into the air. Many of his ribs were broken and one lung was perforated. I went twice to the hospital to visit Raymond, pray with him, and assure him of our love. It was so sad to see him on a respirator and unable to talk to us. His situation was critical, and death seemed imminent. We later returned to the hospital and found Raymond heavily sedated, but the doctor and nurse said there was still hope. The community united in their support and prayers for Raymond. The next morning around ten o'clock, Ray's father called and told us the good news: their son was doing better. There was no immediate danger of death. Before leaving Toronto as planned, I returned to the hospital once more to say good-bye to Raymond and his parents. I showed Ray's father how to make the sign of the cross on Ray's forehead. He had never done this before and cried as he signed his son in the name of the Father, the Son, and the Holy Spirit. A father's blessing can be so healing.

God spoke clearly to me and to the L'Arche Daybreak community through this critical incident requiring pastoral care. During my nine days at Daybreak, I came to feel like an intimate part of the intense joys and sorrows of this community of care. I developed a deep love for the core members and their assistants, who received me with such warm hospitality. They did not hide anything from me. They allowed me to see their fears and their love. I felt deeply grateful for having been part of it all. As I reflected on this tender time over the next several months, I came to see how God had granted me the first glimpse of a new vocation and a place where I could grow into his purposes for me. God used that time to plant the seeds at L'Arche Daybreak for my future pastoral ministry there. The Daybreak community also reflected on our time together and discerned that it would be good to call me to be their pastor. A year later, after what might be called a double discernment, I joined the community as an assistant and resident priest and pastor.

In retrospect, many of the good and important things that have happened to me in life were completely unexpected. And many things that I thought would happen to me did not occur. As I reflect on this reality, it is clear that God is present in the events of my life, yet I act and speak as if I am in control. But if the future is not in my hands, then I have all the more reason to stay in the present and give honor and glory to God from where I am, trusting that God is the God of life who makes everything new. Who knows where you or I will be next year on June 7th? So why worry about it? God will surprise us.

Thomas Merton also viewed the critical events of his life as signposts pointing to the will of God. For example, after his first visit to Gethsemani Abbey in 1941, Merton wrote in his journal: "I desire only one thing: to love God . . . to follow his will. . . . Could it ever possibly mean that I might someday become a monk in this monastery?" Later, he wrote: "Why doesn't this idea of the Trappists leave me?" Reflecting on this persistent feeling and idea led him to interpret it as a sign to which he should pay attention.[2]

Merton's early preoccupation was with writing, and his struggle concerned whether he could do so if he left Harlem for the monastery. "Perhaps what I am afraid of is to write and be rejected. . . . Perhaps I cling to my independence, to the chance to write, to go where I like in the world." In prayerful discernment, he concluded, "If God wants me to write, I can write anywhere. . . . But going to the Monastery is exciting; it fills me with awe and desire. I return to the idea again and again: 'Give up everything!'" Two weeks later, he reported to Gethsemani to begin his life as a monk.

Small, seemingly insignificant events, ideas, and life circumstances can become occasions to discern God's will and calling in your life. Both inner and outer events and circumstances can be read and interpreted as signposts leading to a deeper understanding of the way the Spirit of God is working in our daily lives.

The more we reflect on this, the clearer it becomes that we cannot really understand God's providential work in us. In the final analysis, all we have are signs that lead us to suspect something unspeakably great. "As it is written, 'What no eye has seen, nor ear has heard, nor the human heart conceived, what God has prepared for those who love him'" (1 Cor. 2:9). Though we see as through a dark glass, we do see something. We have the freedom and responsibility to look at our lives with the eyes of faith and a heart of trust, believing that God cares and is active in our lives.

CURRENT EVENTS MAY CONTAIN
DIVINE MESSAGES FOR THE WORLD

Merton also interpreted the critical and current events happening in the world at large as signs from God, not only for himself but for the world. For example, a year after World War II broke out in 1939, Merton entered the Trappist Order. Premonitions of the war and its ominous beginning preoccupied him intensely, as his books and diaries make clear. In his discernment process, he began to understand the gripping power of destruction all around him as more clearly an invitation to voluntarily become nothing and withdraw from the world. The national craving to conquer more land and obtain more goods became for him a call to detach from possessions and go naked through the rest of life. The blind violence that would tear the world apart became for him an appeal to follow the path of nonviolence and accept the consequences. On June 16, 1940, he wrote in his diary:

> Therefore, if I don't pretend, like other people, to understand the war, I do know this much: that the knowledge of what is going on only makes it seem desperately important to be voluntarily poor, to get rid of all possessions this instant. I am scared, sometimes, to own anything, even a name, let alone coin, or shares in the oil, the munitions, the airplane factories. I am scared to take a proprietary interest in anything, for fear that my love of what I own may be killing somebody somewhere.[3]

Merton saw clearly that voluntary poverty not only prevents violence but also frees one to work for peace in the midst of danger. Detachment and displacement also offer a unique opportunity to stand without fear in a violent world. As he writes in *My Argument with the Gestapo:*

I know I am in danger, but how can I be afraid of danger? If I remember I am nothing, I will know the danger can take nothing from me. . . . Yes, I am afraid, because I forget that I am nothing. If I remembered that I have nothing called my own that will not be lost anyway, that only what is not mine but God's will ever live, then I would not fear so many false fears.[4]

Given his spiritual ability to discern God's will and vocation for himself in the midst of a huge event, as well as its ominous message for the world, as "signs of the times," it is not surprising that Merton is seen as one of the most important writers on peace and nonviolence, one who constantly questions what detachment and *kenosis,* self-emptying, mean for the modern person.

Detachment, for Merton, does not mean shirking one's responsibilities. Rather, it is a radical stance in the world that makes it possible to move unafraid into the center of evil and not be destroyed by it. If you claim nothing as your own, including your own life, you can expose the illusion of control and the false basis of war and violence by refusing any compromise with evil. Thus the self-emptied person is the true revolutionary in the world. How might we stand aside from all our demands and desires in this age of consumerism and militarism and seek peace within—peace for our immediate community and peace in the world?

When millions of people experience the same event or series of critical events in the world, these events become, according to Merton, *occasions* to discern the signs of the times. And the messages they contain are not only for the individual but also for the community of faith and the world at large. What were the signs in the critical events of his day? During the years Merton spent in the Trappist monastery, he wrote at least thirty-five books, in addition to his many letters, diaries, and journals. When we consider his enormous work, it appears that his greatest power and insight went into his commentary on the concrete happenings and current events of the day, born out of silence and discernment. It is instructive to see how he read the signs of the times and discerned what God was trying to say and do in the world.[5]

In *Conjectures of a Guilty Bystander*, Merton offers his vision of the 1960s and the shocking and tumultuous events of his day. When racial strife burst out with all its vehemence, when the conscience of America suffered under the Vietnam War, when poverty became a national nightmare, Merton was a voice to which people listened to find some light in the darkness and some clarity amid the confusion of the time.

From 1960 to 1968, Merton followed the news about the killing of children in Birmingham and civil rights workers in Mississippi; the killing of ministers in Selma, Alabama; the burning of churches in the South; the riots in Watts, Newark, Chicago, and Cleveland; the long march from Selma to Montgomery and the dramatic march to Washington, where Martin Luther King Jr. proclaimed his dream. These were critical *events* that followed upon each other in quick succession and severed the unity of a great land. He did not seek to turn away from the news or mute its horror; he sought to see beyond the raw facts to glimpse the power of God at work in even the most tumultuous times in our personal and cultural lives.

In 1963, the president of the United States was assassinated: in 1964–65, Black leaders were killed by snipers. The figure of Dr. King came forward as a sign of hope, and thousands walked with him in nonviolent protest. But when he was shot down in 1968 and buried in Atlanta, the option of active nonviolence seemed to be buried with him.[6] The hot summer of 1968 began with fires in Detroit and Chicago and a growing fear of chaos. In June 1968, Robert Kennedy, a white leader who could still inspire hope, was assassinated. Murder, hatred, anarchy, chaos, desperation, despair, fear, and anxiety—these were the signs of the times. America fell lame and waited for the end, or for a time of restoration.

Merton did not feel called to leave the garden of Gethsemani for the front lines of the civil rights movement, to join the peace movement, or to actively participate in protests in the streets. Nor did he turn his back on the world with contempt. His task as a monk was to pray and discern, to "unmask the illusion"—first his own illusion, then the illusion in the social order.[7]

For Merton, the fires, destruction, death, and riots of the 1960s pointed to a *kairos*—a historic opportunity for the majority culture to confess their guilt and turn away from the oppression so embedded in the economic and power structures of the day, for the country to set itself right. In *Seeds of Contemplation,* he writes, "The irony is that the Negro . . . is offering the white man a 'message of salvation,' but the white man is so blinded by his self-sufficiency and self-conceit that he does not recognize the peril in which he puts himself by ignoring the offer."[8]

Kairos means that the opportunity is right. It is the right time, the real moment, the critical event, the chance of our lives. When our time becomes *kairos,* it opens up endless new possibilities and offers us a constant opportunity for a change of heart. The events of life—even such dark events as war, famine and flood, violence and murder—are not irreversible fatalities but rather carry within themselves the possibility of becoming a moment of change. To start seeing that the many events of our day, week, or year are not *in the way* of our search for a full life but rather *the way to it* is a real experience of conversion.

Much more can be said about how God speaks through the events of our lives and world, and you have divine messages to discern in your own story. By citing examples from the life of Thomas Merton, as well as from my own experience, I have tried to show how books, nature, people, and critical events can be signs along life's way. They do not give a full explanation of our calling, but they are expressions of it. They may not reveal with complete clarity God's will, but they do form the context for discernment. As signs and signals, they provide daily guidance, prompt personal decision making, support action, and offer confirmations of the new direction we see so vaguely.

It may be a bit disappointing initially that when we look for clear answers to the burning questions in our lives, we are left only with titles of books, experiences in nature, names of people, and a series of seemingly random events. They seem too lean and superficial to constitute a doctrine of discernment. God cannot be caught once and for all or contained for all time in a system of titles, names, nature, and events. But God lets himself be *suspected!* Therefore, when we pray to God or search for God in silence, we learn to recognize him in the many little ideas, meetings, happenings, signs, and wonders along the way.

EXERCISES FOR DEEPER DISCERNMENT

1. Take a piece of paper and draw a foundation stone at the base of the page to represent your birth. Write on the stone your date of birth and the circumstances. Then build upon that stone, adding other stones to represent the major events of your life. Feel free to add the joyful events as well as those that were full of sorrow or failure. When you have finished this part of the exercise, go back and add notations about the major cultural or world events that have taken place during your life: political changes, wars, major natural events, and so on. When you have finished, look at the whole picture and reflect on this question: What might God be doing in my life and in the world?

2. Record in your journal, and share in your small group, how God has spoken to you through a critical event, perhaps one from the previous exercise that revealed a message for you. After listening to the group, reflect and share what you have learned or noticed about the way God works in all our lives.

PART THREE

Discerning Vocation,

Presence, Identity,

and Time

SEVEN

Test the Call: Discerning Vocation

Before I can tell my life what I want to do with it,
I must listen to my life telling me who I am.
—*Parker Palmer*

What is God calling me to do? Where is God calling me to go?
Where do I belong? These persistent questions have circled back
to the center of my prayers many times during my life.

From the beginning, two inner voices have been speaking to
me: one saying, "Henri, be sure you make it on your own. Be sure
you become an independent person. Be sure I can be proud of
you," and another voice saying, "Henri, whatever you are going to
do, even if you don't do anything very interesting in the eyes of
the world, be sure you stay close to the heart of Jesus; be sure you
stay close to the love of God."

I'm sure we all hear these voices to some degree—one that says, "Make something of your life; find a good career," and one that says, "Be sure you never lose touch with your vocation." There's a struggle, a tension there.

At first, I tried to resolve this by becoming a sort of hyphenated priest—a priest-psychologist. People would say, "We don't really like having priests around," and I could reply, "Oh well, I'm a psychologist. I'm clearly in touch with things, so don't laugh at me." I tried hard to keep those two voices together—the voice calling me upward toward success in the church and academy and the voice calling me downward into solidarity with the poor and vulnerable.

Early in life, I pleased my father and mother immensely by studying, then teaching, and then becoming somewhat well known, by going to Notre Dame, Yale, and Harvard. I pleased a lot of people by doing so and also pleased myself. But somewhere on the way up, I wondered if I was still in touch with my vocation. I began noticing this when I found myself speaking to thousands of people about humility and at the same time wondering what they were thinking of me.

I didn't feel peaceful. Actually, I felt lonely. I didn't know where I belonged. I was pretty good on the platform, but not always that good in my own heart. I began to wonder if perhaps my career hadn't gotten in the way of my vocation. So I began to pray: "Lord Jesus, let me know where you want me to go, and I will follow you. But please be clear about it." I prayed this over and over. I have returned to this prayer at many times and seasons in my life, whenever I felt God calling me to a new place of ministry.

"What does God want from me?" is a question we all ask, not once and for all but throughout our lives. Should I get a job or go back to school, get ordained or do lay ministry, teach or preach, work in another country or closer to home, get married or stay single, have a family or join a community? There are many facets to a life fully committed to God's will and way.

What I tell others who ask these questions, and remind myself with surprising conviction, is this: "God has a very special role for you to fulfill. God wants you to stay close to his heart and to let him guide you. You will know what you are called to do when you have to know it." New vocations are full of promise. Something very important is in store for us. There is a hidden treasure to discover.

ALL ARE CALLED TO MINISTRY

Each of us has a mission in life. Jesus prays to his Father for his followers, saying, "As you have sent me into the world, so I have sent them into the world" (John 17:18 NRSV). We seldom fully realize that we are sent to fulfill God-given tasks. We act as if we have to choose how, where, and with whom to live. We act as if we were simply dropped down in creation and have to decide how to entertain ourselves until we die. But we were sent into the world by God, just as Jesus was. Once we start living our lives with that conviction, we will soon know what we were sent to do. These tasks may be very specialized, or they may be the general task of loving one another in everyday life.

The gospel tells the story about Andrew and another disciple of John who followed Jesus. Jesus said: "What are you looking for?" They said: "Rabbi, where do you live?" When Jesus said, "Come and see," they stayed with him. Later Andrew shared with his brother Simon what they had seen and heard, and so Simon came to Jesus (John 1:38–42). This story offers three important verbs to reflect upon in discerning how God is calling: to *look* for, to *stay*, and to *share*. When we search for God, stay with him, and share what we have seen with others, we become aware of the unique way Jesus calls us.

During my longest stay at the Abbey of the Genesee in 1974, I read an article about the new pipeline being built in Alaska. The state of Alaska had become the land of the oil rush, with the same kind of effects as the gold rush had in the previous century. In Alaska, I thought, there are conglomerations of adventures, new searchers for immediate wealth, new bars and crimes, and shoot-outs by "crude-oil men" living quite the life there. They must be tough but lonely, and they probably have great spiritual needs. I imagined traveling there and starting some sort of Ecumenical Camp Mission. I imagined myself preaching and doing liturgy in the barracks, followed by long talks with the workmen around campfires and in taverns. I remembered previous spiritual adventures of preaching to people working on a dam in the Pyrenees and driving in "chapel trucks" through West Germany to give retreats for Catholic refugees from East Germany when I was a young man. Old memories from long ago, yet they do not seem so long ago.

Though I was spiritually drawn to the idea of ministry in the wild, how did I know if God was calling me to be a priest in Fairbanks? Thomas Merton thought about going to Alaska to live as a hermit. That was one of his daydreams while he traveled through India as a pilgrim in 1968. I know that sometimes a call from God is planted in our imagination, and if it persists we need to bring others into our discernment process to test if it is something to pursue or just a diversion. My particular desire to go to Alaska turned out to be a diversion. Conversation with friends helped me see that my vocation lay elsewhere. I returned to my teaching career, which remained fruitful for many years.

Testing a Call to Live and Work in Latin America Among the Poor

After spending ten years teaching spiritual theology at Yale Divinity School, I felt free to confront directly a question that had haunted me for so long: Why do I feel so strongly drawn to the poor of Latin America? Unlike my idea of ministry in Alaska, this attraction to live in Latin America was not short-lived. I can only say that I never gave up the urge and deep conviction that I must learn Spanish somehow, sometime. I have never been able to fully explain this conviction to myself or to anyone else. Why? I don't know. I hope that I will know before I die. There must be a meaning for such a strange passion!

I read an article about the Maryknoll communities in Peru that gave me a strong sense of déjà vu. Paul Blustein described Father Peter Ruggere's encounter with an infant girl who suffered from malnutrition "and most certainly won't live beyond her fifth birthday. When the priest swoops the baby into his arms, gurgling endearments in Spanish, the child neither laughs nor cries, but merely gazes blankly at him through filmy brown eyes." When I read this, I sensed a pull to Peru all over again and realized that he was speaking about my future neighbors in Lima. I knew I had to go and see for myself what God was doing in Peru and seek to discover if God had a place of service there for me.

After long wrestling with vocational questions, I finally left Yale, where I had been well celebrated and affirmed, to test a new call. I visited my Trappist friends at the Abbey of the Genesee in upstate New York and started to prepare myself for more systematic discernment of a possible vocation in Latin America. For me, it was important to say good-bye, to let go of what is past before looking forward to a totally new ministry and vocation. It seemed paradoxical, but the expressions of friendship from former students and colleagues at Yale and the deep personal conversations gave me a profound sense of mission. I realized that I was going not just because it seemed like a good idea but because those who loved me most sent me on my way with affection, support, and prayers. The more I realized I was truly loved, the more I felt the inner freedom to go in peace and let all inner debate about motivation subside.

My friend John Vesey, whom I had met in Bolivia in 1972, and who had come from Brooklyn to New Haven to help me pack, expressed his enthusiasm for my decision to return to Bolivia for more language training and to join the Maryknoll fathers in Peru. Through our friendship and my trust in his strong sense of God's guidance, I was convinced more than ever that it was good for me to go. Sometimes the way to know where you are called to be is to go where you feel you need to go and be present in that place. Soon you will know if that place is where God wants you.

In October 1981, I flew to Lima, Peru, to get to know my Maryknoll hosts, and from there to Cochabamba, Bolivia, for a three-month course designed to improve my Spanish. I kept a daily journal during this transition period to record and impose some order on the myriad impressions, feelings, ideas, and encounters that filled my heart on this six-month journey toward discernment.[1] But, most of all, I tried to find an answer to the question, does God call me to live and work in Latin America in the years to come?

From the moment I entered Peru, I felt a deep love for this country. Walking through the busy streets and looking at the men, women, and children, I had the strange emotion of homecoming. "This is where I belong. This is where I must be. This is home." For me, it was a day of comfort and consolation, a day on which the decision to come to this country was affirmed. Peru, like most of Latin America, exhibits impressive wealth and degrading poverty, splendid flowers and dusty roads, loving people and cruel tortures, smiling children and soldiers who kill. Here, in the struggle, we search for God's treasure amid the paradoxes and sorrow.

While at Yale, I had taught a course on the wisdom of the desert fathers of fourth-century Egypt. Reading again the sayings from the desert in the context of Peru gave them an unusual power. One story goes like this: One day Abba Arsenius asked an old Egyptian man about what he was thinking. Someone noticed this and said: "Abba Arsenius, why is a person like you, who has such a great knowledge of Greek and Latin, asking a peasant like this about his thoughts?" He replied: "Indeed, I have learned the knowledge of Latin and Greek, yet I have not learned even the alphabet of this peasant."

To learn the alphabet of the peasant is the first task of a pastoral worker called to minister among the poor. The *campesinos* of Peru have a great treasure to share, and they will share it with those who want to listen and learn.

Those who are truly called to serve the poor in another country, I learned in Latin America, are people who hunt for the divine treasure hidden in the hearts of the people to whom they want to make the good news known. They always expect to see the beauty and truth of God shining through those with whom they live and work. The Spirit of God in us recognizes God in the world. The eyes and ears by which we see God in others are in fact spiritual sensitivities that allow us to receive our neighbors as messengers of God. Thus, to go to the poor is to go to the Lord. I had to discover whether I could see God and serve God over many years in Peru.

AM I CALLED TO LIVE AMONG THE POOR?

The big question for me was, Can I truly live with the poor? For a little less than a year, I lived with the poor in Latin America and shared their lives to some extent, but I am far from poor. I like to eat good meals and have time to read books and take walks. I like showers with hot water. I like to sleep in from time to time, take a regular day off, and travel. So my living with the poor hardly makes me poor. Some feel that to be in ministry with the poor, you should be no different from them; others say that such solidarity is not realistic or even authentic. My ministry experience in Latin America showed me that I was physically, mentally, and spiritually unable to survive without the opportunity to break away from it all once in a while. The functions of

life, which previously hardly required attention in my apartment
in the United States—washing, cooking, writing, cleaning, and
so on—were complicated and time consuming in the community
house in Peru. The winds covered everything with thick layers
of dust; water had to be boiled to be drinkable; there was seldom
a moment of privacy, with kids walking in and out all the time;
and thousands of loud noises made silence a faraway dream. I
loved being there and fell in love with people who were extremely
poor, but I was also glad to escape it whenever opportunities
arose for me to be with others who were more like me.

A certain realism is necessary to fulfill a call to work and live
among the poor. You have to accept your own history and limitations. You have to remind yourself that Jesus said, "Blessed are
the poor," not blessed are those who try to help the poor. At the
same time, you have to deal with the gospel call to downward
mobility, accepting that the way of Christ is a self-emptying way.
What that means in your own concrete situation will probably
remain a lifelong question.

My vocational questions did not become easier to answer when
I arrived in Latin America. There were days when I felt deeply
attracted to the idea of living and working among the poor. But
there were other days when I was so overwhelmed by the language and culture, the daily struggles and never-ending nature
of the pastoral work that I could hardly imagine feeling at home.
My emotions swung back and forth within hours between great
enthusiasm and deep self-doubt. I dealt with this hardship by
talking with as many people as I could about my plans and non-
plans to stay or go.

I allowed myself more time to let things develop in me before
making a decision. It was a gradual process of discernment. I
trusted I would know what to do when I felt at home and experienced a call from God and from the people. I had to bring my
search more intentionally into the presence of God and pray more
directly for light.

March 26, 1982, proved to be a critical day for me. I met again with Father Matias Siebenaller, a priest from Luxembourg serving as pastor in Caja de Agua, one of Lima's barrios. We talked in the morning for three full hours! I felt in my heart the many pieces of my puzzle coming together. He offered concrete suggestions with warmth and support, and gave me a true sense of being called. He offered his own parish as a good place to try out my ideas about forming a little community of radical hospitality, mutual ministry, contemplation, and action in the midst of a barrio.

Matias also felt strongly that I had been in Peru long enough to make a firm decision to stay or go. Another period of search and fervent prayer would be unnecessary. While it was not possible to be completely certain and making decisions always entails risk, I needed to stay until I had enough information to make up my mind. Matias urged me not to cut off all contact with the academic world in the United States was important. While he stressed that I should commit myself firmly to the Peruvian church and be willing to work in the service of that church, he also felt that it would be good to continue to communicate, through writing and lecturing, with the world from which I had come.

My morning discussion with Matias began to give me a sense of closure. I sensed my stay in Peru was coming to an end, my impressions of ministry starting to show patterns for future work. I felt called to be part of a radically hospitable community of faith, but it was not likely to be in South America. I did not feel I could or should live there permanently. That day, I gained a sense of harmony, of things fitting together, of belonging—and, yes, vocational clarity. To find my vocation, I had to come to Peru as a necessary step in the discernment process even if it did not become my new home.

Through a series of circumstances, conversations, and contemplative impressions over a six-month period, I became acutely aware that my desire to live and work with the poor in Latin America was not matched with a concrete call. I knew that the university was no longer the place to live out my vocation, but I also started to see that neither God nor God's people were asking me to make Bolivia, Peru, Guatemala, or Nicaragua my permanent home. My experiences there, as exciting and rewarding as they were, never led me to that deep inner imperative that forms the center of a true call.

As I was trying to discern an answer to the question, does God call me to live and work in Latin America? I gradually realized that the word *gracias* that came from the lips of the people contained the answer. All is grace. Light and water, shelter and food, work and free time, children, parents, and grandparents, birth and death—it is all given to us. Our very first vocation is to receive these gifts and say thanks. If I have any vocation in Latin America, it is the vocation to receive from the people the gifts they have to offer us and to bring these gifts back up north for our own conversion and healing.

Once I knew that I was not called to live among the poor in Latin America, my task became clear to return to North America and offer my voice to tell others about the needs and beauty of my friends in Peru. As my friend, Jean Vanier later told me that my task was to speak for the poor and not so much to be engaged in direct service to the people. My primary gifts and calling were to write, speak, and be in solidarity with my friends in Latin America. I did not have the grace to live there long term. And you must have the gifts and grace to fulfill a task for it to be a vocational call from God.

Although I was not called to stay long in Latin America, I met someone who was. Her story of discovering her call illustrates the need to grow into the questions that arise when we sense the pull to explore a new way of life in the world. Pilar is a Mexican assistant who lived for two years with people with mental disabilities at L'Arche in Trosly, France, before feeling called to live and work among the poor in Latin America. Pilar combines a deep spiritual life with a strong talent for leadership. She is gentle and forceful, prayerful and active, God-centered and deeply committed to fighting for the rights of the poor. "I have always felt called to work with the poor," she told me. "Now I know for certain that people with disabilities are the poor I am called to be with."

The question for Pilar was not "Who?" or "What?" but "Where?" Jean Vanier had told her to think about Brazil and Guatemala as places to start a new L'Arche community in Central America. Pilar listened carefully and finally said, "I don't want to go somewhere just to have my own project. It must be clear to me that God calls me there. Otherwise it can't bear fruit."

She proposed that we spend some time together in a little chapel to pray for more clarity. As we prayed silently, I felt deep joy at being part of something very fragile, very new, and very hopeful.

What I learned from testing a call in Latin America is that my broader vocation is simply to enjoy God's presence, do God's will, and be grateful wherever I am. The question of where to live and what to do is really insignificant compared to the question of how to keep the eyes of my heart focused on the Lord. I can be teaching at Yale, working in the bakery at the Genesee Abbey, walking with poor children in Peru, or writing a book, and still feel totally useless. Or I can do these same things and know that I am fulfilling my call. There is no such thing as the right place or the right job. I can be miserable or joyful, restless or at peace, in all situations. It is a simple truth that came to me in a time when I had to decide about my future. Living in Lima or not for five, ten, or twenty years was no great decision. Turning to the Lord fully, unconditionally, and without fear *is*. He reminds me that I have no lasting dwelling on this earth, that I am a traveler on the way to a sacred place where God holds me in the palm of his hand. This deeper awareness sets me free to be a pilgrim, to pray without ceasing, and to be grateful.

Road to Daybreak: A Call to Come Home

I returned from Peru to teach at Harvard, knowing that I was called to bear witness to God's concern for the poor and oppressed, especially in Latin America. I also felt called to be part of a radically hospitable community that served the poor, but I still did not understand where that community might be. Yet, as had happened in the past, God spoke to me through the people who spoke to me, planting seeds and preparing the way for a future not yet revealed.

Soon after moving to Cambridge, I received a knock on my door one morning from someone I did not know. This was during a difficult time, when I was longing for a community where I could live a life of prayer and ministry that seemed impossible for me at Harvard. I opened the door and saw a young woman standing there.

"Are you Henri Nouwen?"

"Yes, I am."

"I've come to bring you the greetings of Jean Vanier," she continued.

I knew of Jean Vanier as the founder of the L'Arche community in France and that he worked with mentally handicapped people. I had read one of his books and included it in my required reading list for a course I was teaching on the spiritual life. But I had not yet met the man.

I said, "Oh, that's nice. Thank you. What can I do for you?"

"No, no, no," she answered. "I've come to bring you the greetings of Jean Vanier."

Again I said, "Thank you, that's nice. Do you want me to talk somewhere or write something or give a lecture?"

"No, no," she insisted. "I just wanted you to know that Jean Vanier sends his greetings."

I learned this woman's name was Jan Risee, and when she had gone, I sat in my chair and thought: "This is something special.

Somehow God is answering my prayer, bringing a message and calling me to something new." I wasn't asked to take a new job or do another project. I wasn't asked to be useful to anybody. I simply was invited to come to know another human being who had heard of me. There was something so unexpected and surprising about this encounter.

Almost three years after Jan Risee first visited me, I finally met Jean Vanier.

Jean and I met quietly at a silent retreat during which no words were spoken. At the end, Jean said to me in a very simple and undemanding way, "Henri, maybe our community of handicapped people can offer you a home, a place where you will be really safe, where you can meet God in a whole new way."

He didn't ask me to be useful; he didn't ask me to work for handicapped people; he didn't say he needed another priest. He simply said, "Maybe we can offer you a home." I knew then that he spoke in God's name.

Gradually I realized that I had to take that call seriously and began to explore a new possible vocation among people with mental challenges. I again left the university and went to the L'Arche community at Trosly-Breuil in France. After spending a year with this community of mentally disabled people and their assistants, who try to live in the spirit of the Beatitudes, I responded to the call to become a priest at Daybreak, which is a L'Arche community near Toronto, a community of about one hundred: fifty handicapped people and fifty assistants. I could not have imagined that I would end up in a community in Canada rather than one in South America. My discernment time in Peru showed me more about who I am and my limitations, and prepared me to later hear the call to meet Jean Vanier and explore joining the L'Arche community. These long months and years were leading me where I could not have predicted.

VOCATION—A PURPOSE TO FULFILL

In retrospect, I knew I was called to live not in Latin America but in Toronto, North America. And my permanent home was to be found not as a university professor at Yale or Harvard but as pastor of the Daybreak community. At first it seemed that there could be no greater contrast than between Lima and Toronto—between the poor of Pamplona Alta and the mentally challenged people of Daybreak; between the intense struggle for survival in South America and the safe, well-protected life of our L'Arche community; between the fierce theological discussions about Liberation Theology and the gentle sharing sessions about our communal life. But as I look back at my six months in Latin America and the search for a vocation that so occupied me there, I can say without the slightest doubt that without the experiences I recorded in my journal I would not be where I am today.

In Lima, Peru, I discerned God's preferential concern for the poor and grew in the conviction that I, too, had to choose that option. It was there that I heard the clear call to dedicate my future to the life of a shepherd. It was there that I discovered for the first time that those who are marginalized by our society carry within them a great treasure. And it was in Lima that I learned that without prayer and community all my pastoral activities would end up in fruitless burnout.

I can now see that my desire to leave the university and live in community among the poor was a God-given desire, though one whose concrete realization required some real purification. Only gradually did I discover that God's call was in fact a divine response to the deepest desire of my own heart: the desire to find a home among God's poor.

It took a long time to understand that I belong to Daybreak community. I thought my vocation was simply to serve the poor, but I learned that my deeper vocation is to announce God's love for all people. I also became aware that my final destination is not a place; it is God's eternal embrace. With that clarity, I can be with anyone at any place and enjoy the goodness, beauty, and love I see while remaining at home with my God, who sent me into the world to speak and act in Jesus's name. Discerning my vocation has taken me around the world and required much prayer and conversation with many others. Yet every step was part of reaffirming who I am in God and that I have a purpose to fulfill which is uniquely mine. We all do.

EXERCISES FOR DEEPER DISCERNMENT

1. What "inner voices" have been part of your life thus far? Henri heard the call to be successful, and it was in tension with his call to remain close to the heart of Jesus and the poor. Can you name the tensions you feel between the expectations placed on you by others and your desire to fully follow God's purposes for you? Once you have named these different voices, try having a conversation with each of them to help you clarify how these differing expectations affect what you do with your life energies.

2. Nouwen learned in Peru that he could not live long term among the very poor. He was used to leisure time and comforts not possible when living in solidarity with his neighbors in Lima. What limitations or previous commitments do you have? How does this factor into the call God has placed on your life? Can you accept them as a part of the discernment process? What might you need to do to affirm who you are—strengths and weaknesses—as God's called and gifted person?

3. Eventually Henri discerned the *who* (people with disabilities), the *what* (announcing the gifts of the poor and the love of God), and the *where* (the Daybreak community) of his

final vocation. Which of these three parts of your own call do you have clarity about and which are you exploring? The various aspects of your call fit together like a puzzle when you discover who you are to serve, what you are to do, and where you will find your true home. What do you know for sure, and what remains unclear? Journal about each of these parts of your vocation. Share them with your small group or spiritual director.

EIGHT

Open Your Heart: Discerning
Divine Presence

In God we live and move and have our being.
—*Acts 17:28*

There is that of God in every person; and that of God in everything.

—*Quaker tradition of the inner light*

Every morning, alone or in the company of others, I spend at least one hour in quiet prayer and meditation. I say every morning, but there are exceptions. Fatigue, busyness, and preoccupation often serve as arguments for not praying. Yet without this one hour a day for God, my life loses its coherence, and I start experiencing my days as a series of random incidents and accidents rather than divine appointments and encounters.

My daily hour with God is not a time of deep prayer in which I contemplate the divine mysteries or feel a special closeness to God. On the contrary, it is full of distractions, inner restlessness, confusion, and boredom. It seldom, if ever, pleases my senses. Even though I do not feel God's love the way I feel a human embrace, even though I do not hear a voice as I hear human words of consolation, even though I do not see a smile like I see a human face, still the Lord speaks to me, looks at me, and embraces me there. The way I become aware of God's presence is in that remarkable desire to return to that quiet place and be there without any real satisfaction. And I notice, maybe only retrospectively, that my days and weeks are different when they are held together by these regular and "useless" times. God is greater than my senses, greater than my thoughts, greater than my heart. I do believe that God touches me in places that are hidden even to myself. And I do believe that when I pray I am in touch with the divine presence reflected in my heart.

The presence of God is often subtle, small, quiet, and hidden. "A shoot shall sprout from the stump of Jesse, and from his roots a bud shall blossom" (Isa. 11:1–2 NAB). Our salvation comes from something small, tender, and vulnerable, something hardly noticeable. The Lord, who is the creator of the universe, comes to us in smallness, weakness, and hiddenness. When I have no eyes for the small signs of God's presence—the smile of a baby, the carefree play of children, the words of encouragement and gestures of love offered by friends—I remain spiritually blind. The promise of divine presence is hidden in the shoot that sprouts from the stump.

BE PRESENT TO THE PRESENCE IN PRAYER

In his wonderful little booklet "Beginning to Pray," Anthony Bloom describes how Staretz Silouan, the simple Russian peasant who died in 1938 on Mount Athos, prayed for his neighbor, Nicholas, who worked with him in the monastery workshop:

> In the beginning I prayed with tears of compassion for Nicholas, for his young wife, for the little child, but as I was praying, the sense of the divine presence began to grow on me and I lost sight of Nicholas, his wife, his child, his needs, their village and I could be aware only of God and I was drawn by the sense of the divine presence deeper and deeper until, all of a sudden, at the heart of this presence, I met a divine love holding Nicholas, his wife and his child and now it was with the love of God that I began to pray for them again, but again I was drawn into the deep and in the depths of this I again found the divine love.[1]

As Archbishop Bloom tells the story, Father Silouan worked in the monastery workshops alongside the many peasants who came for a year or two, hoping to make enough money to start a family, build a home, or buy land to plant crops. Bloom writes,

> One day the other monks who were in charge of other workshops said, "Father Silouan, how is it that the people who work in your workshops work so well even though you never supervise them, while we spend our time looking after them and they try continuously to cheat us in their work?" Father Silouan said, "I don't know. I can only tell you what I do about it. When I come in the morning, I never come without having prayed for these people, and I come with my heart filled with compassion and with love for them, and when I walk into the workshop I have tears

in my soul for love of them. And then I give them the task they have to perform in the day, and as long as they will work I will pray for them. So I go into my cell and I begin to pray about each of them individually. I take my stand before God and I say, 'O Lord, remember Nicholas [and the others].'"[2]

What is this inner experience of divine presence that some-times occurs when we pray with compassion for others? How can we cultivate it in our daily lives? The scriptural answer, I think, is found in the experience of two disciples of Jesus on the road to Emmaus.

DID NOT OUR HEARTS BURN WITHIN US?

Listen carefully to this passage to discern the real presence of the one who walks beside us on the road. You may wish to read it aloud to hear things your eyes might miss:

Now that same day two of them were going to a village called Emmaus, about seven miles from Jerusalem. They were talking with each other about everything that had happened. As they talked and discussed these things with each other, Jesus himself came up and walked along with them; but they were kept from recognizing him.

He asked them, "What are you discussing together as you walk along?"

They stood still, their faces downcast. One of them, named Cleopas, asked him, "Are you only a visitor to Jeru-salem and do not know the things that have happened there in these days?"

"What things?" he asked.

"About Jesus of Nazareth," they replied. "He was a prophet,

powerful in word and deed before God and all the people. The chief priests and our rulers handed him over to be sentenced to death, and they crucified him; but we had hoped that he was the one who was going to redeem Israel. . . ."

He said to them, "How foolish you are, and how slow of heart to believe all that the prophets have spoken! Did not the Christ have to suffer these things and then enter his glory?" And beginning with Moses and all the Prophets, he explained to them what was said in all the Scriptures concerning himself.

As they approached the village to which they were going, Jesus acted on as if he were going farther. But they urged him strongly, "Stay with us, for it is nearly evening; the day is almost over." So he went in to stay with them.

When he was at the table with them, he took bread, gave thanks, broke it and began to give it to them. Then their eyes were opened and they recognized him, and he disappeared from their sight. They asked each other, "Were not our hearts burning within us while he talked with us on the road and opened the Scriptures to us?"

They got up and returned at once to Jerusalem. There they found the Eleven and those with them, assembled together and saying, "It is true! The Lord has risen and has appeared to Simon." Then the two told what had happened on the way, and how Jesus was recognized by them when he broke the bread. (Luke 24:13–36 NIV).

The two people walking on the road together have lost their way. Their faces are sad and downcast, their lives are encircled by darkness, and their conversation draws them deeper into despair. They had put their hope in Jesus, who they thought was the one to redeem Israel. But apparently they feared they had been mistaken, for he had been condemned by the authorities, executed, and taken from their sides.

When I imagine myself on that dark road to Emmaus, I see myself in a depressing dialogue with the other disciple. Sometimes we are consumed in our own personal concerns and dramas. We are poisoning each other's capacity for love and transformation. No longer able to experience the inner vitality and outer confidence to make a difference in the world, we are in danger of spiritual death. Unable to recognize the gift of God in ourselves or in the other, we are lost. Our despair has put us in the tomb.

Jesus walks with us on the road, unrecognized; he joins us in our sadness and despair. Having been in the tomb for three days, he understands what it means to be stuck there. He listens to our story of confusion, disorientation, deep grief and loss of direction, human failure, and inner darkness. Yes, he is with us in our lostness.

Finally, he speaks. Jesus speaks from the tomb. He reveals from firsthand knowledge that God's love is stronger than our despair, that God's faithfulness reaches beyond the experience of divine absence, and that God leads those whom he loves through the darkness of the tomb into the light of the resurrection. That's why hearts that have grown cold can burn with joy once again.

But there is even more to this story and ours. The story of the disciples on the road to Emmaus is not just about overcoming sorrow or despair in difficult times. It is a gospel story that reveals a spiritual pattern for discovering the real presence of Christ on our road of life. This pattern of discerning God's hidden presence involves at least four spiritual practices: 1) *interpreting scripture,* or theological reflection; 2) *staying,* sometimes called abiding or remaining in prayer; 3) *breaking bread,* or recognizing the presence of Christ in the Eucharist; and 4) *remembering* Jesus, or the "burning heart" experience. These components form a biblically grounded and traditionally understood practice of discerning the divine presence in daily life.

Interpreting Scripture

Speaking to the disciples on the road to Emmaus, Jesus asks, "Did not the Christ have to suffer these things and then enter his glory?" (Luke 24:26 NIV). These words are among the best known of the Gospels, for they radically change our view of suffering. Pain and suffering are no longer obstacles to the glory of eternal life, they have become the inevitable way to it.

In teaching the disciples about the suffering of Abraham, Moses, and the prophets, Jesus gradually shows them that what depresses them most—the suffering of the friend they thought to be the Messiah—has become the source of new life. When Jesus opens the scriptures to them, their hearts are set afire. That which made them give up hope and return to their old way of life is converted. That which prevented them from recognizing the Messiah on the road is transformed. They are now ready to receive the new thing God is doing in the world. Rather than expecting a life without disappointments or moments of depression, they see that Jesus comes to meet us right in those moments, with hope and the potential for a new way of seeing and believing.

In the life of the church, the "service of the Word" at each Eucharist seeks to put us in touch with this mysterious presence. The readings from the Old and New Testaments and the homily that follows are given to us to discern Christ's presence as he walks with us in our sadness and joy. The Eucharistic presence is first of all presence through the Word. Without presence through the Word, we aren't able to recognize the divine presence in the breaking of the bread. It is important to remember that interpreting scripture is best done with others. Just reading a bit of scripture in isolation does not allow us to enter fully into the mystery of Christ's promise to be present when two or more are gathered together.

Staying

The stranger had listened to *them;* this allowed them to listen to *him* as he interpreted the scriptures. In the process, their hearts were restored. They rediscovered the gift of love in their innermost being. This brings new life, new hope, and new energy, ushering in a whole new world.

The stranger has become a friend, and the disciples want him to stay longer. He doesn't ask for an invitation. He doesn't beg for a place to stay. In fact, he acts as if he wants to go on. But they insist that he come in; they even press him to stay with them. He accepts their invitation to "stay."

The word *stay* is related to the verb *to abide,* and it has a spiritual meaning in the Gospels. It refers to an *inner staying* that is liberating and life-giving. Remember what Jesus said earlier in his words of farewell to the disciples: "As a branch cannot bear fruit by itself but must *remain* [stay] part of the vine, neither can you unless you *remain* in me" (John 15:4). The great final promise of Jesus is: "I am with you always, to the very end of the age" (Matt. 28:20 NIV). Staying with Jesus and he with us requires walking the road together, not turning back, anticipating seeing Jesus in unexpected ways in our hearts.

Breaking Bread

After Jesus enters their home with them and "stays" with them, they suddenly recognize him at table when he says the blessing. Jesus had a particular way of taking bread, blessing it, breaking the bread, and offering it to others. So simple, so ordinary, so obvious, and still, so very different! The veil that had prevented them from seeing him on the road is suddenly lifted when he blesses and breaks bread, eats and drinks with them at table. Now they know who he is, and that he is still with them.

Eucharist—in both the ordinary and sacramental meaning of the term—is recognition. It is the full realization that the one who takes, blesses, breaks, and gives is the one who from the beginning of time has desired to enter into communion with us. To do so is to receive and recognize the gift of divine presence. It is helpful to notice that this thanksgiving meal on the way to Emmaus was not a church service but a meal with people who were tired from a journey. They recognized Jesus in the homey hospitality of deep compassion and companionship.

Remembering

"Then their eyes were opened and they recognized him," but as soon as they recognize him, he disappears from their sight. In the same moment as the two friends recognize him in the breaking of the bread, he is no longer there with them. Precisely when he becomes most spiritually present to them, he also becomes physically absent. Here we touch one of the most sacred aspects of Eucharistic theology: the deepest communion with Jesus is a communion that happens in his absence. This is a mystery of faith. Christ is with us and yet we await his full return.

After Jesus vanishes from their sight, they ask each other, "Were not our hearts burning within us while he talked with us on the road and opened the Scriptures to us?" Mysteriously, after this encounter in which their eyes and hearts are opened, the two disciples no longer need his physical presence to know that he remains with them. They can now "remember" him who dwells within them.

The miracle that happened with these two disciples is something that can happen to us today as well. Not long ago I had such an encounter. Certain events in my life were weighing heavily on me and pulling me into a depression. But God sent someone to me—an unexpected friend in whom I could easily put my trust. I shared with him the details of the events that caused my dark state of mind. He listened for a long time, and then gently showed me that I was on the same road as he, that I was being led through much pain to a new place. This new place was actually one that had been created in the gospel encounter between the two disciples and the stranger. When I opened my heart to this new reality, I was no longer an isolated and lonely individual who returns to the old place of his youth. I was no longer alone; I had found a friend, a companion, a voice of love. As I confessed, a heavy burden fell away from me. Later, when we had a meal together, I knew that God had sent his angel to me to offer me comfort and consolation and turn my despair into hope.

The great event on the road to Emmaus is the new communion. Someone listened, understood, and became a friend. The two lost disciples found a new place where the events that had led to sadness were being transformed into events that brought joy. They recognized that they were no longer alone. After breaking bread with them, Jesus vanished from their side because he no longer needed to be there with them. Now they knew him "by heart" and were set free to return to Jerusalem and bring the good news to others. There is reciprocity to receiving God's presence. We are comforted and restored to offer comfort and restoration to another who is struggling on the road.

Remembering Jesus—reweaving hope and meaning through an encounter with the risen Christ—freed the disciples to return to their community to raise hope: "They got up and returned at once to Jerusalem. There they found the Eleven and those with them, assembled together . . . then the two told what had happened on the way and how Jesus was recognized by them when he broke the bread."

Discerning the divine presence through scripture reading (*lectio divina*), staying with Christ (abiding in his presence in prayer) in the breaking of bread (*Eucharist*), and remembering Jesus (*anamnesis*) results in the burning heart experience (of divine memory, or *memoria Christi*). These four movements in the road to Emmaus story form the structure of the church's Eucharistic celebration of the divine presence that we discern or recognize in the Sacrament. Each time we approach the table in worship, we can hope to touch the story of the road to Emmaus, represented and remembered as a present reality.

IN THE EUCHARIST WE RE-MEMBER CHRIST

I have written earlier about *lectio divina,* or sacred reading,[3] but there is something more about the breaking of bread and remembering Christ in relation to discernment. In the celebration of the Lord's Supper, we discern the real presence of the risen Christ among us, not only in the bread and wine but at the center of our lives, the core of our very being, the heart of our community, and the heart of creation. Father John Eudes once said in a homily at the Abbey of the Genesee:

> Lord is truly present—yet in a quiet, subtle, unobtrusive, and elusive way. Christ lives in us, physically even, but not in the same physical way that other elements are present in the human body. A spiritually transcendent physical presence is what characterizes the Eucharist. It is already the other world present in this one when we re-member Christ.

Philosophers and Christian theologians often use the term *anamnesis* to explore the reality of what happens when we recall and remember Christ, not as a historical person from the past but as someone fully in the present moment.

"There is a kind of enclave in our world of space and time." Father John continues, "Christ is really here—and yet his physical presence is not characterized by the same limitations of space and time that we know."

The philosopher Heidegger applied the term *Dasein* to the reality behind the appearance: "Behind the appearance is a reality of presence that is distinguishable, perceptively apart from the pure physical being there."[4] I don't want to retreat into abstractions here but hope to emphasize that Christian hope rests on the reality that the spirit and presence of Jesus transcend time. We believe that the risen Christ, the spirit of Jesus, can be encountered anytime and anywhere.[5]

DISCERNMENT AND SACRED MEMORY

Saint Augustine used the term *memoria Dei*, the memory of God, to express the idea that God is eternally present in humanity through sacred memory. According to Saint Basil, the memory of God is spiritual *gnosis*—true knowledge of God that is found in the heart. When we "remember" God, we are touching the divine nature within our very souls. For God knows us from eternity to eternity, has loved us with an unconditional love, and has carved us on the palm of his hands. Through the spiritual practice of learning to be aware and expectant, we *remember* God as love and ourselves as God's beloved.

The early church fathers wrote often of the "memory of God" to emphasize the presence of God in all humanity. Human beings discover God because we recognize God's reflection in our most inward and intimate self. And thus we long to be fully reunited with the source of the reflection, whom we remember. There is a deep desire in the faithful for reunion with God, the source of life, strength.[6]

There is also a uniquely Christian concept of *memoria Christi* that is reflected in sacred history and the life of faith. God became human and so entered into history. The birth of Christ—his death, resurrection, and ascension—took place in time. We can speak about Jesus in the past tense—he came, he lived, he died—and we can also speak about the memory of Christ's advent in the present moment. We celebrate the *memoria Christi* in the Eucharist when we remember his life and recognize his presence among us "until he comes again." In the Christian sense of the word, the knowledge and memory of God are given to all, received in baptism, and celebrated in the breaking of bread whenever the body of Christ is gathered.[7]

Both concepts of memory—the Neoplatonic (philosophical) and the Christian (historical)—are worth exploring in depth so as to come to a deeper understanding of prayer and discernment. A good place to start is the works of Saint Augustine, especially the *Confessions* and his work on the Trinity.

THE PAIN, POWER, AND MYSTERY OF MEMORY

Reading and thinking with the Christians of the past is a helpful way to widen our view of faith and solidify our trust that God is at work in often mysterious ways. Yet, in times of crisis, many of us can't think much about the workings of God because we are consumed with recollecting and remembering our past pain in the experience of the present moment. We go back again and again to re-look and re-feel hurtful times. The memory of unhappy events in my personal life can lead to painful and often damaging emotions. Memory of past actions can lead to *remorse*, whose root word, *mordere*, means literally "to bite"! Remorse is the biting sensation that causes me to say: "How could I do such a thing? Why did I let myself go this way? How stupid of me! How could I let that happen?" Remorse can keep me awake at night, make me restless during the day, and take away my peace of mind.

The Pain of Memory
The pain of memory can also make me ashamed. *Shame* makes me aware of my surroundings and susceptible to the negative assessments of others. In shame I say, "What will others say about me? What will they think? Have I made a fool of myself? Will they laugh at me because of what I did or because of who I am?"

Then there is *guilt*. Guilt makes me realize that I have hurt someone else. In guilt I say, "I did harm to my friends. I have broken something precious. I have wounded another."

When I relate to my past with remorse, shame, or guilt, the danger is that I will harden my heart and be unable to discern the divine presence within and without. When my heart is hardened, it is closed, unavailable, and cold. A hardened heart is a heart in which remorse has turned into morbid introspection, shame into low self-esteem, and guilt into defensiveness. When I keep thinking about myself and my motivations, constantly comparing myself with others and trying to defend my behavior, I am becoming more and more self-centered, and the divine love diminishes in me. The pair on the road to Emmaus almost missed the presence of Christ because they were so focused on their loss. They are much like us. It is easy to miss seeing that we are not alone when defensiveness and despair are sown in our hearts.

These three reactions to painful memories make us unhappy and may hinder or stifle the spiritual life. Awakening to the presence of Christ can heal the wounds of my memory. Opening our hearts to the divine presence in the present moment, thus transforming our emotions and healing our memories, is a great challenge of the spiritual life. The memory of the image of God in the soul can turn my stone heart into a heart of flesh, making it flexible, receptive, open, and free.

Remembering Christ transforms remorse into contrition, for "a broken and contrite heart, O God, you will not despise" (Ps. 51:17 NRSV). Remembrance of Christ converts shame to compassion, which allows us to reach out to others who share our struggles. And the memory of Christ prevents guilt from overwhelming us and makes us receptive to forgiveness. The memory of Christ is thus a healing, spiritually therapeutic memory. By remembering my life and struggles in the light of Christ's presence, my past is redeemed and can become an occasion for thanksgiving and praise.

The Power of Memory

Although memory sometimes brings the painful past closer in the present, it also creates a deep desire for reunion with those I remember and for reconciliation with what is past. The power of memory is not only that it allows me to relive the past but also that it transforms the past in the present and the future.

For example, I feel closely related to many friends who have died. I remember them in faith and expectation that I will see them again. The memory of those I love makes me desire a reunion, a new encounter face-to-face. In some mysterious way, in the absence of a loved one from the past, I sense a spiritual closeness in the present that prepares me for a reunion in the future that is deeper and fuller than their presence in the past or their presence in the present.

I can even say that I must remember those in the past to make full reunion possible in the future. Their memory is in a certain sense preparation for seeing them again. Remembering grandparents, parents, brothers and sisters, and friends who have died or gone away is not just some sentimental, pious custom of those who can't move on; it is the continuation of a relationship that still exists and has yet to come to fulfillment. Indeed it is the Spirit of Christ that tells us there is a coming reunion more profound than the relationship in the past or present.

Would it be true to say that remembering a friend or family member in death allows for a spiritual communion to develop that was not fully realized during their physical presence? Can we say that memory unites us in spirit with a connection deeper than physical union? If so, we must confess that bodily presence not only reveals the real person to us but also hides the real person from us. One's physical presence both reveals and hides the deeper, more authentic self that I desire to encounter. In physical absence, the spiritual presence is no longer blocked. This mystery sheds new light on life and death. Being fully alive means being truly present to God and others as best we can. Dying means not only leaving but also entering into a more intimate relationship and a deeper spiritual presence than was possible during physical life.

The Mystery of Memory

If remembering a loved one who has died sometimes brings me closer to the spiritual reality or essence of his or her presence in memory, then the memory of Christ likewise brings me closer to Jesus than even his physical presence on earth could do. His death, his leaving me behind, has made it possible to receive his Spirit and to live in and with him always. The memory of Christ brings me into spiritual communion with him and with his body, the church. As Saint Paul—the only apostle who had not been with Jesus physically before his death and resurrection—said with deep conviction, "For to me, living is Christ, and dying is gain" (Phil. 1:21 NRSV).

This insight gives power and meaning to the words of Jesus: "It is good for you that I go because unless I go, the Advocate will not come" (John 16:7). In the memory of Jesus, we receive his Spirit and enter into a mysterious communion with him that is deeper and more intimate than if he had been with us physically and historically.

In every Eucharist, the people of God proclaim the mystery of faith: "Christ has died, Christ is risen, Christ will come again." In the very act of *remembering* Christ, we not only recall the past reality but somehow see Christ in the future event. We discern Christ in the present moment when we cease to be afraid.

REMEMBER: WE ARE NOT ALONE

Let me sum up this chapter on seeking the divine presence in the midst of life's disappointments and hardships with another example from scripture. Do you remember the gospel story about the disciples in the boat on the Sea of Galilee (Matt. 14:22–33)? During the night, the disciples encounter a storm, and they are afraid. Jesus comes to them, walking on the water. They think it's a ghost, and they are terrified. Jesus tells them, "Take heart, it is I; do not be afraid."

Peter replies, "Lord, if it's you, command me to come to you on the water." Jesus says, "Come." Peter gets out of the boat and begins walking on the water toward Jesus. But when Peter notices the strong wind and waves, he begins to sink. He cries out to the Lord, and Jesus immediately reaches out his hand and catches Peter, asking, "Why did you doubt?" As they climb into the boat together, the storm ceases. Then those in the boat worship him, saying, "Truly you are the Son of God."

This is a story about moving from fear to discernment in the present moment, a story we all need to hear. So much is going on in our lives: new directions, old fears, apprehensions, and great uncertainties. Always, there is sadness and joy, fear and love, resentment and gratitude; there is nervousness about next week, next month, next year. Yes, there is so much going on beneath our feet that we are wondering if we can keep walking on all these waves. But Jesus is with us here and now. As long as Peter keeps his eyes fixed on Jesus, he can walk on the water. Problems are small and fears bearable when we know who calls us. The Lord looks into us, smiles, stretches out both his hands, and invites us to get out of the boat: "Come to me, be not afraid."

We will not succeed if we stay in the boat. We will not survive if we look down at the waves. But we do not have to look down and drown. Jesus calls us to look up and forward to the one who stands in the midst of the storm. He is with us now, he will be with us tomorrow, and he will still be there in our near and far future. In the midst of all the storms, he is the quiet presence; in the midst of all our doubts and fears, he is the safe dwelling place; in the midst of all our restlessness, he is our home. Why feel anxious in the *presence* when he is reaching out his arms to us? Why worry about the future when Christ says, "I will be with you until the end of time" (Matt. 28:20)?

Please, Lord, join me on the road, enter into my closed room, and take my foolishness away. Open my mind and heart to the great mystery of your active presence in my life, and give me the courage to help others discover your presence in their lives. Amen.

EXERCISES FOR DEEPER DISCERNMENT

1. Reflect on the road to Emmaus story in Luke 24. If you have a small group or prayer partner, discuss four ways we can experience divine presence on the road of life.

2. Read scripture. Take time to read the story of Emmaus Road aloud several times, letting aspects of the Word speak to you and move from your head into your heart. This requires slowing down and listening to what God is saying through scripture.

3. Break bread (Eucharist). Share a simple meal with your spiritual friends and remember how eating, hospitality, and Christ's presence are all connected.

4. Abide. "Stay" in the present moment. Try not to run from your pain or dwell in the past. Actively work during this week to keep your mind and heart in the present moment, where you are not alone.

5. Remember Christ. Take communion this week. Pay attention to the way you are invited to meet with Christ at the table while you walk your own road to Emmaus.

NINE

Remember Who You Are: Discerning Identity

You cannot tell me who I am and I cannot tell you who
you are.
If you do not know your own identity, who is going to
identify you?

—*Thomas Merton*

Who am I? This is a core question that every person asks and answers throughout life. Naming ourselves, seeing the shifting roles
we play during our lives, and seeking to live by the values and beliefs at the heart of our existence are lifelong challenges. Are we
who others say we are? Are we what we achieve and can put on
a business card or stamp into bronze? Who am I? Who are we?

As Christians, brothers and sisters, we can shout with joy that we are like Jesus, who became like us in every respect, yet without sin. According to the Letter to the Hebrews:

> Since the children have flesh and blood, he too shared in their humanity so that by his death he might break the power of him who holds the power of death—that is, the devil—and free those who all their lives were held in slavery by their fear of death. For surely it is not angels he helps, but Abraham's descendants. For this reason he had to be made like them, fully human in every way, in order that he might become a merciful and faithful high priest in service to God, and that he might make atonement for the sins of the people. Because he himself suffered when he was tempted, he is able to help those who are being tempted. (Hebrews 2:14–18, NIV)

If this is true, and I believe it is, then we, too, are God's beloved sons and daughters. Between Jesus and us there is no essential difference. We are as much God's children as Jesus is a child of God. Through Jesus we are made "joint heirs"—all that God taught to Jesus has been shared with those who follow after him. The term *adopted children* (in Romans 8:15–17; 9:4) does not mean being second in importance to Jesus, who is the "only begotten son of God." It refers to us having been made children of God to enjoy the full inheritance of Jesus and participate in the divine life.

MORE THAN OURSELVES

Jesus's entire mission on earth was to lead us into his own divine life. In no way does Jesus want us to know less or do less than he himself knows or does. We are called to be like him, and to do the things he did. Indeed, Jesus said, "whoever believes in me will do the works I have been doing, and they will do even greater things than these . . ." (John 14:12 NIV). Jesus wants our whole being to be where he is, our deepest identity to be grounded in his, and our spiritual life to be in sync with his, so that we can live our lives as he lived his—fully in God.

The Second Letter of Peter states that God's divine power has been given to us to transcend human mortality by becoming "partakers of the divine nature" (2 Pet. 1:4 KJV). In other words, we are more than ourselves. We are both human and divine, just as Christ was both divine and human! Jesus affirmed this truth in John 10:30–34, when he told the religious leaders of his day, "I and my Father are one." When they accused him of blasphemy, "because you, being a man, make yourself God," he added insult to injury by claiming to be the Son of God. Quoting Psalm 82:6, Jesus said: "Is it not written in your law, 'I said, "You are 'gods'; you are all sons of the Most High.'"[1]

WE ARE THE BELOVED

At the core of my faith belongs the conviction that we are the beloved sons and daughters of God. What the Father said to Jesus the Son, God also says to us: "You are my Son, the Beloved; with you I am well pleased"(Luke 3:22 NRSV).

Dear friends, I want you to hear this: what is said of Jesus is said of you. I know this can be hard to affirm. You are the beloved daughter or son of God. Can you believe it? Can you hear it not only in your head through your physical ears but in your gut, hear it so that your whole life can be turned around? Go to the scriptures and read: "I have loved you with an everlasting love. I have written your name in the palm of my hand from all eternity. I have molded you in the depths of the earth and knitted you in your mother's womb. I love you. I embrace you. You are mine and

I am yours and you belong to me." You have to hear this, because if you can hear this divine voice speak to you from all eternity, then your life will become more and more the life of the beloved, because that is who you are.

When you start believing this, this spiritual knowledge will grow until it transforms your daily life. You will still have rejections and you will still have pain and losses, but you will live them no longer as a person searching for his or her identity. You will live them as the beloved. You will live your pain and anguish, your successes and failures, as one who knows who you are.

And that's not easy. Most of us constantly fail to claim the truth of who we truly are.

Claiming Our Belovedness

Not long after I arrived as a priest at L'Arche Daybreak community, I had a powerful experience of offering the blessing of belovedness to another. Shortly before I started a prayer service, Janet, a member of our community, said to me: "Henri, can you give me a blessing?" I responded in a somewhat automatic way by tracing with my thumb the sign of the cross on her forehead. "No, that doesn't work," she said. "I want a real blessing!" I suddenly became aware of the inadequacy of my response and said, "Oh, I am sorry, let me give you a real blessing when we are all together for the prayer service." She nodded with a smile, and I realized that something special was required of me.

After the service, when about thirty people were sitting on the floor, I said, "Janet has asked me for a special blessing. She feels she needs that now." Janet stood up and walked toward me. I stood up and opened my arms to welcome Janet as she walked up and laid her head on my chest. Putting my hands on her shoulders, the sleeves of my robe enveloped her. I looked at her and said, "Janet, I want you to know that you are God's beloved daughter. You are precious in God's eyes. Your beautiful smile, your kindness to the people in your house, and all the good things you do show us what a beautiful human being you are. I know you feel a little low these days and that there is some sadness in your heart, but *I want you to remember who you are:* a very special person, deeply loved by God and all the people who are here with you."

As I said these words, Janet raised her head and looked at me; she smiled and said, "Thanks, Henri. That's so much better than the first one."

The blessings we give each other are expressions of the blessing that rests on us from all eternity. It is the ultimate compliment, the deepest affirmation of our true identity in God.

The truth is that God loved us before we were born and will love us still after we have died. God molded us in the depths of the earth. God knitted us together in our mothers' wombs. God has inscribed us on the palm of his hand. Every hair on our heads is numbered and counted by God. We are held by God in an everlasting embrace. We belong to God from eternity to eternity. Indeed, we are God's daughters and sons. As beloved children, our core identity is secure in the memory of God. Whether we do anything worthwhile, prove anything important, or give anything of value, God still loves us unconditionally. It is a strong, vital, and active fatherly and motherly kind of love that holds us safe and affirms our worth, wherever we go and whatever we do.

Our first and most important spiritual task is to claim God's unconditional love for ourselves. To remember who we truly are in the memory of God. Whether we feel it or not, whether we comprehend it or not, we can have spiritual knowledge in the heart—a deep assurance that passes understanding—that we are God's beloved.

This is not an easy identity to claim because to deserve being loved our society requires us to be successful, popular, or powerful. But God does not require our success, popularity, or power in order to love us. Once we discern our identity and accept God's unconditional love, we are free to live in the world without being owned by the world. We can forgive those who hurt or disappoint us without letting bitterness, jealousy, or resentment enter our hearts. The most beautiful fruit of *claiming your belovedness* is a joy that allows us to share God's unconditional love with others. Strange as it may sound, we can become *like God* for others.

From the moment we claim the truth of being the beloved, we are faced with the call to *become who we are.* Becoming the beloved, remembering who we are, is the greatest *blessing* in our lives! In Latin, to bless is *benedicere,* which means "speaking (*dictio*) well (*bene*)" or saying good things of someone. I need to hear good things said of me, and I know you have the same need. I need to learn to speak well of the work God is doing in my life and yours, not with self-congratulation but with humble awareness of divine activity.

To give someone a blessing is the most significant affirmation we can offer. It is more than a phrase of appreciation; it is more than praising another's gifts or good deeds. To give a blessing is to affirm another's core identity, to say yes to a person's belovedness. Claiming our belovedness does not come easily for many of us. There are competing voices we hear. When one voice says we're nothing but a sinner and another voice says we are the beloved of God, we are called to discern the spirits and follow the inner voice of love.[2]

RESTORED TO OUR TRUE SELVES

Jesus came into the world to give us spiritual life (*zoe*), a new identity, a true self—one no longer dependent on the fragile structures of the world but rather on the eternal love between the Father and the Son, between a loving parent and much-wanted child, a love that is called the Holy Spirit. It is as if we have been wandering in a foreign land looking for peace and purpose in our lives and a true sense of who we are. Jesus stands in our midst and beckons us home so that we can be restored to our true selves.

When we belong to God, as children, as brothers and sisters of Jesus, breathing the Spirit who binds Father and Son, Creator and Redeemer, in a perfect unity of love, then we have spiritual knowledge of God's heart that enables us to know who we truly are and see the world as God sees it.

What do I mean by seeing the world the way God sees it? This is important for discerning—for seeing rightly. In the Gospels, there are many examples of Jesus not giving a direct answer to questions put to him by his disciples and others. (For example, the mother of James and John asks whether her two sons might sit one at the right hand and the other at the left hand of Jesus in his kingdom, and Jesus responds, "Are you able to drink the cup that I am about to drink?" [Matt. 20:20–23].) He does this not because he has no patience with them but because their questions are the wrong questions; they are not the questions that live in God's heart but belong instead to the fearful, anxious world of those who do not know who they are.

As we come to know, more and more, that we belong to God and are part of the life of God, we also come to know the heart of God. Some of our frantic questions—What must I do? How can I get what I need?—fade away when we come closer to God's heart. Then we begin to hear the questions and see the struggles that we encounter from that sacred place. In God, we gain new ears to hear, new eyes to see, and new hearts to discern what is really happening. Concerns that, in the past, completely occupied our minds lose their meaning. Distinctions that seemed so very important to us dissolve when we look at them from our vantage point in God. What seemed a reason to fear no longer holds us in its power; what made us travel far and wide no longer drives us. Instead, our being is filled with a deep desire to see God's will be done on earth as in heaven.

REMEMBER WHO YOU ARE

When the truth of our identity begins to descend from our minds into our hearts, we may not feel peace and joy! How easy it is to reject part of you as not really yourself and claim only your ideal self as your real self. Can you and I remember that we are the beloved of God when we fail? When we hurt someone else? Even then, we are God's beloved called to remember that beneath our woundedness or frailty is the deeper call to live out of the inexhaustible riches of God's love.

Often, as the desert fathers and mothers and the contemplatives from the Christian tradition affirm, in solitude and meditation the dark and wounded side of us that is still in need of healing often asks for attention and has to be acknowledged as just as much a part of us as our idealized selves. We all have the deceptive tendency to live selectively, choosing to see only those experiences we can identify with as our real experiences and pushing the rest aside. By bringing the whole self to our attention, we not only claim our dark side but also change our ego ideal, the persona or idealized self that is only part of who we are. In a way, in the stillness we cultivate, we become free to stand as we are before God and transcend our limited view of ourselves.

The ego ideal is often made up of self-created expectations and aspirations regarding intelligence, career, physical beauty, moral stature, and so on. The mystery of life, however, is not only that we have a dark side which we want to deny but also that we are better than our own ego ideal! Our true identity is found in God, who created us in the divine image. We are bearers of God's image and spirit. That is the revelation of God within our innermost self.

Often in quiet meditation and reflection we discover that we are more than our individual selves and come to realize who we really are. We slowly learn to see, within our very own hearts, the reflection of the one who breathed life into us. There we come to the *remembrance* of God, who loved us before we were born and before we could love ourselves or try to prove ourselves worthy of love. The truth about ourselves is that we are more than ourselves, more than what we can think or express, more than our physical presence, more than our personality and character. The problem with the excessive reliance on psychology today (and I am a psychologist) is that we tend to give it the last word. But the beauty of psychological awareness is that it can point beyond the character qualities it describes to the person it reveals. Beneath any diagnosis or mental health problem, there is a person who carries God inside. Psychology can give us helpful language for the varied parts of who we are, but we need theology to remind us that we can never be defined by personality or any disorder. We are defined by something deeper and wider than those aspects. This is what is meant when we speak about the soul—that identity where we are most personal and most Godlike.

LIVING OUR TRUE IDENTITY

It is a real struggle to claim our belovedness. Living in the midst of a demanding, pulling and pushing world makes it difficult to remember who we are *in God* and how to live this divine life here and now. Our identities are so wrapped up in the structures and spirit of the world that we live as though we were who the world says we are: rich or poor, able or disabled, good or bad, emotionally stable or vulnerable.

What helped me along the way was an encounter I had with people with disabilities in France. When I first arrived there, I was quite exhausted from hard times and ambitious work, and I needed a rest. When I met people who not only didn't know me but weren't capable of or interested in evaluating me or my accomplishments and nonetheless welcomed me with deep and sincere affection, a new place opened up in me. Their unconditional acceptance broke through my self-rejection and gave me a glimpse of a love that was deeper than my rejecting self. I call it an experience of that "first love" of God from eternity to eternity. The love of vulnerable people who showed me daily affirmation just for being who I was—an exhausted professor and writer and priest who wanted to love others fully—set me on a journey to remember who I was from God's point of view.

Not long after my visit to France, I visited Ukraine, where I spoke at a retreat on the importance of discerning identity—of "claiming our belovedness" and "proclaiming to others their belovedness" as daughters and sons of God. A young Ukrainian came up to me with Thomas à Kempis's *Imitation of Christ* in his hand and showed me the text that says that we are nothing, and that we can live a good spiritual life only when we never forget our nothingness. He was quite perplexed about my positive view of the human person. Staying within his own frame of reference, I explained to him that God had "looked down on the humiliation of his servants" and lifted us up to greatness by revealing to us that we are as beloved as his own son, Jesus.

I tried to convey to him that we are called to live not from the place where we think of ourselves as nothing—useless or sinful—but from the place of our rebirth, the place where we can claim our new identity as the chosen children of God. He tried to understand but was far from truly believing it. I think this young man is not alone. Many Christians are taught that they are unworthy and can never merit God's love. While it is true that we will never earn God's love, that does not mean for us to forget that God came in Jesus to give us fullness of life. We can grow into that truth, for it is a mystery of the kind of love that is really beyond all imagination.

That young man was reading in that wonderful book, *Imitation of Christ,* about one aspect of our identity. that we need God and can't make God love us. I hoped he would also discover in his own tradition, that Ukranian Christianity has made enormous contributions to the Christian contemplative tradition, especially with its emphasis on the in-breaking light of Mount Tabor and the prayer of the heart. There is great beauty in this tradition because it celebrates God's grace in the face of human sinfulness. Christians in the West have much to learn from their Eastern brothers and sisters in this regard.

The awareness of human sinfulness is often diminished in the West. Many people feel they are good enough and have no need for God. On the other hand, human depravity is stressed too much in some Christian traditions, at least from my perspective. The gospel proclaims human freedom and dignity more than human enslavement and depravity. What is needed is a balance of biblical values and emphasis on the empowering quality of the gospel. The spiritual values of humility, long suffering, endurance, and obedience are to be affirmed alongside self-reliance, freedom, proclamation, mission, and authority. The gospel that proclaims the intrinsic worth, sacred value, and essential dignity of human beings encourages our work for equal rights, good housing, good medical care, and good education, and our fight for justice and peace in the world.

So who am I? Who are you? We are God's beloved ones, bearers of the divine image and human beings capable of glory and goodness as well as harm and alienation. We need to hear again and again that we are the beloved of God and that Jesus guides us in the way of being the beloved. He shows us in ever more profound ways how to listen to God, to speak God's words, and to perform the works that God has commissioned. Jesus says clearly to set no bounds to your love, just as your heavenly Father sets none to his (Matt. 5:43–48). Jesus calls us to make our whole lives a life in communion with the Father, whether we eat, sleep, pray, play, speak, or act, so that in all our thoughts, words, and actions we reveal to the world we live in God's immense love for all his children—a love that embraces all people. When we understand the mystery that we are loved not for what we do but because of who God says we are, we are free to love others in a similar way. Discerning what to do and who to serve changes radically when we know we love from God's love and serve from God's heart. The very places where we might be called open wider as we understand that announcing God's love for the poor, the wounded, and the sick is at the heart of all responses to the truth and that we all are the beloved ones of God.

EXERCISES FOR DEEPER DISCERNMENT

1. When you read the words, "Between Jesus and us there is no essential difference. We are as much God's children as Jesus is a child of God," what was your first response? Is this what you have been taught? Journal about your initial reaction and what that might help you discern about your own beloved-ness before God.

2. The young man in Ukraine believed that we "can live a good spiritual life only when we never forget our nothingness." If he came to you, what would you say? Write him a letter describing how you understand God's vision of you and how that influences the way you seek to live in the world. (If you are in a small group, share these letters and discuss how your vision of God's view of you influences your self-understanding and sense of call.)

3. Henri describes Janet's request to receive a special blessing. What words of blessing do you long to hear? If you were to ask someone to offer a benediction saying good things of you, what would you hope they would say? Would you be able to accept those things? In your small group, offer words of blessing to one another. Seek to open your hearts to hear what others say without dismissing the good words too quickly.

4. For a week, start and end your day with the words, "I am the beloved of God." Journal at the end of the week about how these words sounded to you in your heart at the beginning and end of the week. How do they affect your openness to discerning God's healing work in your life?

TEN

Know the Time: When to Act, When to Wait, When to Be Led

For everything there is a season,
and a time for every purpose under heaven.
—*Ecclesiastes* 3:1

How do we know when to act, when to wait? How will we know when it is our time to lead rather than our time to follow? Discernment calls us to spiritual understanding but also to action. We first seek God's presence, listen to the books, people, and signs in daily life, and explore vocation; but then there is always a moment when we must choose and step out.

In his book *Conjectures of a Guilty Bystander,* Thomas Merton wrote:

There is a time for action, a time for "commitment," but never for total involvement in the intricacies of a movement. There is a moment of innocence and kairos, when action makes a great deal of sense. There is [also] a time to listen, in the active life as everywhere else, and the better part of action is waiting, not knowing what next, and not having a glib answer.[1]

To act or not to act. To wait or to move. To speak or remain silent. All of these can be faithful acts. Living in the presence of God and trusting the Spirit helps us discern right action in everyday life.

A TIME TO ACT

At Yale Divinity School during Holy Week one year, a small group of the theology students invited me to join them in a prayer vigil at Electric Boat, the nuclear submarine shipyard in Groton, Connecticut. There, a new nuclear Trident submarine was being built and would be named *Corpus Christi* (the body of Christ)! On Holy Thursday, we all gathered in preparation for a Good Friday peace action. For many months, these hardworking, intelligent, deeply believing students had come together once a week to pray. During these times, they had gradually grown into a community of people able to listen to God's guidance. Together they had read the scriptures, spoken about their fears and apprehensions, and tried to find words to express their deepest convictions. They found their Christian call to announce God's love to be at odds with naming and commissioning a weapon of war as "the body of Christ."

What a paradox! The body of Christ is called to build us up in love. Finally, they decided to publicly protest what the government considered necessary for the protection of the nation. Some felt that they were called to break the law and let themselves be arrested. Others, including myself, were less sure about that. But everyone was ignited by the inner call to say no to death and yes to the God of life in a way that was exceptional and visible, with a hope that others would respond. The group discerned that it was time to act.

On Good Friday, we went to Groton to witness for peace in front of the administration building of Electric Boat. The leaders of the group asked me to lead the community in the stations of the cross[2] on the streets of Groton in prayerful resistance to the nuclear arms race. We prayed fervently with words and songs, as well as in silence. We heard the story of Jesus's suffering in a way that we could not have heard it in any church. I felt a deep awareness that prayer was no longer a passive religious event taking place in a sanctuary but an active, even dangerous and subversive act that challenged the very structures of the world. Moreover, the words I had so often spoken from pulpits about death and resurrection, about suffering and new life, suddenly received a new power—a power to unambiguously condemn death and call forth life.[3] It was a pivotal moment for me. I could no longer speak about the peace of Christ without resisting the drumbeat of war and systemic violence. Worship could not remain a private affair for the faithful. My worship took me increasingly to where people suffered at the hands of the powerful.

Many years later, I went to Central America and witnessed the immense agony of the people, which called for immediate response. I came to the painful awareness that the Word of Jesus which had been brought to Central America at the beginning of the sixteenth century by Catholic missionaries had sometimes broken and tortured the very people who were called to be witnesses to its reconciling power. There were Christians imprisoning Christians, Christians torturing Christians, and Christians murdering Christians, and an immense darkness covered the incarnate Word.[4] The body of Christ was fractured, and it was harming its varied parts. I know Christ weeps when his body fails to love.

As I recognized the tragic political, economic, military, and religious conflicts in Nicaragua, Guatemala, and Peru, many of them involving the church and government, I was challenged to become more active in my spirituality. Upon my return to North America, I engaged in a peacemaking tour to call attention to the grave injustices committed in the name of Christ and democracy and to testify that God was calling us to spiritual and political action.[5] I couldn't speak about love in a general way, then stand back and watch as government and religious leaders ignored the suffering of the very poor. I returned from Central America with a conviction that startled my audiences and sometimes me. "What the U.S. government and, indirectly, the U.S. people are doing in Central America is unjust, illegal, and immoral," I felt led to proclaim to church and university audiences. "It is unjust because we intervene in a country that in no way threatens us; it is illegal because we break every existing international law against intervention in an autonomous country; and it is immoral because we inflict destruction, torture, and death on innocent people. 'Christ is risen' means that we are a people of reconciliation, not of division; people who heal, not hurt; people of forgiveness, not of revenge; people of love, not of hate; people of life, not of death."

When it is time to act, we must act with repentance and gratitude. When I joined the protest against the *Corpus Christi*, and as I increasingly felt compelled to remind my friends in North America about the grinding poverty of South America and point out how our northern comforts often were gained by the labors of the very poor, I was often asked why we should take action in favor of civil rights. Why not pray that God will act? I came to understand that I was called to speak on behalf of the voiceless so that they might find hope but also so that the oppressor could be converted. Acting out of discernment will not lead to all persons affirming our actions, but it will point to the call to transformation of our own lives and the society in which we all live.

Why should we act in the peace movement? So we can discover the source of violence in our own hearts. Why act to alleviate hunger? So we can unmask our own greed. Thus all actions for others can become acts of repentance that bring us into growing solidarity with our fellow human beings and so establish the basis for reconciliation. Indeed, God is the one who acts, and by our repentance we can hasten God's action. Here it becomes clear that our action is part of Christ's coming, that in a mysterious way the realization of the new heaven and new earth depends on us.

Action, however, is related not only to repentance but even more to gratitude. Action is a grateful response that flows from our awareness of God's presence in the world. Jesus's entire ministry was one great act of thanksgiving to his Father. It is to active participation in this ministry that we are called. I discovered, in moving more and more into announcing God's love to the poor and widening my sense of vocation to include those with disabilities, that I was following a well-worn path. Peter and Paul traveled from place to place with a relentless energy. Teresa of Avila built convents as if she would never get tired. Martin Luther King Jr. preached, planned, and organized with unquenchable zeal. And Mother Teresa of Calcutta fearlessly hastened the coming of the Lord with her care for the poorest of the poor. Their bold actions were free of compulsion, and consequently were spontaneous responses to the experience of God's active presence in their lives. Our actions, too, can become an overflowing of grateful thanksgiving.

A Time to Wait

At Yale, when it was time to demonstrate against the *Corpus Christi,* I was clear that I had to act. I could not keep silent or still. But there have been many other times when the guidance was not as clear. Whenever there is a lack of clarity or ambiguous circumstances, it is time to wait. Active waiting is essential to the spiritual life. In our mostly active lives and fast-paced culture, waiting is not a popular pastime. It is not something we anticipate or experience with great joy. In fact, most of us consider it a waste of time. Perhaps this is because the culture in which we live is basically saying, "Get going! Do something! Show you are able to make a difference! Don't just sit there and wait." But the paradox of waiting is that it requires full attention to the present moment, with the expectation of what is to come and the patience to learn from the act of waiting.

The disciples have much to teach us about following the way of Jesus. Waiting as a disciple of Jesus is not empty waiting. It is waiting for the promise hidden in our hearts, which makes already present what we are waiting for. In fact, Christians have built-in waiting times throughout the church year. During the season of Advent, we are waiting for the birth of Jesus, manifested in the world and in our hearts during Epiphany. During Lent, we wait in the desert of solitude for new life to be revealed. We wait after Easter for the coming of the Spirit at Pentecost, and after the ascension of Jesus we wait for his coming again. We are always waiting, but it is waiting with the conviction that we have already heard God's promises and seen God's footsteps in Jesus.

Waiting for the fulfillment of God's promises to us allows us to pay full attention to the road on which we are walking. It allows us to keep our eyes fixed on Jesus and to live in God's present moment. Even when we are discerning for the longer term, we are called to follow the guidance we have to pray, be still, live in community, and be of service to those who cross our path. Walking with Jesus keeps us in the present. And this kind of waiting is the opposite of worrying about the future. It's tasting the *presence* to the full in the knowledge that "this is the day that the Lord has made; let us rejoice and be glad in it" (Ps. 118:24 NRSV).

Waiting for the promise always means paying attention to what is happening right now before our eyes and seeing there the first rays of God's glory.

The Psalms are full of this kind of waiting: "My soul is waiting for the Lord. I count on his word. My soul is longing for the Lord more than the watchman for daybreak. (Let the watchman count on daybreak and Israel on the Lord.) Because with the Lord there is mercy and fullness of redemption" (Ps. 130:5–7 Athanasian Grail Psalter version).

The gospels are full of stories of waiting. The story of the birth of Jesus in the Gospel of Luke introduces us to five people who are waiting with expectation—Zechariah and Elizabeth, Mary, Simeon, and Anna. Besides being individuals loved by God, they are representatives of waiting Israel. They are able to wait for the promise to be fulfilled, to wait with attention to the Word, and to wait with hopeful expectation.

Zechariah is waiting in the temple with a sense of promise: "Zechariah, your wife Elizabeth is to bear you a son." Mary, the mother of Jesus, listened to the angel: "You are to conceive and bear a son." She then went to wait in the company of Elizabeth, where she pondered what she had heard and what was foretold. Simeon, the priest in the temple, had been waiting for much of his life to see the Messiah. He waited, trusting that he would not see death before he had seen the Christ (Luke 1:13, 31; and 2:26 JB). Those who were waiting, as the remnant of believing Israel, had each received a promise that gave them courage and allowed them to wait with expectation. Zechariah and Elizabeth, Mary, Simeon, and Anna all were present and attentive to the moment. They were alert and responsive to the voice that spoke to them and said, "Don't be afraid. Something is happening to you. Pay attention."

Mary, especially, was patient and attentive in her waiting. "May it be to me as you have said" (Luke 1:38). This obedient waiting leads to contemplative prayer and lets us enter into the fullness of time. "As for Mary, she treasured all these things and pondered them in her heart" (Luke 2:19).

Waiting with Patience

How do we wait for the promise to be fulfilled? We wait with *patience*. But patience does not mean passivity. Waiting patiently is not like waiting for the bus to come, the rain to stop, or the sun to rise. It is an active waiting in which we live the present moment to the fullest in order to find there the signs of the one we are waiting for.

A waiting person is a patient person. The word *patience* comes from the Latin verb *patior*, which means "to suffer." Waiting patiently is suffering through the present moment, tasting it to the fullest in the belief that something hidden there will manifest itself to us. When we know that we are God's beloved and we are free to live in the house of love, all patience is *co-patience*—suffering with the suffering God, thus suffering and compassion that give birth to new life. "You will be weeping . . . you will be sorrowful, but your sorrow will turn to joy" (John 16:20). Such *co-patience* is not just a chronological sequence but also an experience of the fullness of time, in which the divisions between joy and sadness, fullness and emptiness, presence and absence, and even living and dying are taken away.

The Greek term *hypomone* (translated as "patience, endurance, perseverance, and fortitude") indicates a "dwelling in the moment" (Luke 8:8, 15; 21:16–19). It refers to actively entering into the thick of life. When we are impatient, we experience the present moment as empty and we want to move away from it. Much of our commercial culture skillfully exploits our impatience and tempts us to move toward the "real thing," which is always somewhere else or at some other time.

Impatient living is living according to clock time (*chronos*), which has a merciless objectivity to it. It does not allow for spontaneity or celebration. Patient living is living in the fullness of time (*kairos*), in the knowledge that real life events happen in this fullness. And the great event of God's appearing is recognized in the fullness of time (Mark 1:15).

Patience—an active dwelling in the present moment—is the mother of expectation. A way to rephrase "waiting patiently in expectation" is "standing vulnerable in the presence of our loving God." This is the core of all prayer. It has been helpful to me to realize that, when I pray, I am living my life before God, doing what I know to do, offering my thoughts and actions to the Holy One in expectation that I am being led where I need to go and will be given the courage to do what I need to do because I know who I am in God.

Active waiting is being open to the promise yet to be fulfilled. Patient waiting is staying fully in the present moment. Expectant waiting is trusting that this long process will bear fruit. As a contemporary representative, Simone Weil, writes: "Waiting patiently in expectation is the foundation of the spiritual life."[6]

A TIME TO BE LED

There is a time to act, a time to wait, and a time to be led. When we are young, we want to act and hold everything in our own hands, but when we grow old or more spiritually mature, we learn to wait, to open our hands in prayer and let ourselves be led to "where we would rather not go" (John 21:18). Thus we will come to know the freedom of God's Spirit, which leads to new life, even if the cross is the only sign we see.

When I was at teaching at Harvard, I was invited to visit a friend who was very sick. He was a man fifty-three years old who had lived a very active, useful, faithful, creative life. He was a social activist who had cared deeply for people, especially the poor. When he was fifty, he discovered that he had cancer.

During the three years that followed, he became increasingly disabled.

When I came to see him, he said to me, "Henri, here I am lying in this bed, and I don't even know how to think about being sick." He explained how his whole way of thinking about himself was in terms of action, doing things for people—how his life no longer felt valuable once he became passive and couldn't do anything anymore, not even for himself. "Please help me to think about this situation in a new way," he asked me. "Help me to understand what it means now that all sorts of people are doing things to me over which I have no control."

As we talked, I realized that he was constantly wondering, "How much can I still do?" Somehow my friend had learned to think about himself as a man who was worth only what he was doing. He was tempted to despair because he had cancer and was going to get worse and worse. Eventually, he would die. What could I say to him?

In the context of these thoughts and prayers, we read together a powerful book called *The Stature of Waiting* by W. H. Vanstone. The author writes about Jesus's agony in the Garden of Gethsemane and his way to the cross, and it helped my friend and me to understand better what it means to move from action to passion. This is a kind of waiting that most of us resist and our culture often denies. But it is a reality of the spiritual life. We are given these lives to live in response to God's love, yet our time on earth is one where suffering visits us and we are called to live in compassion, to "suffer with" others. Waiting in a time of sorrow or suffering can be one of the most difficult but also the most fruitful times of life. We step close to the way of Jesus when we step into our own pain and the pain of others. Often we are thrust into suffering; we are handed over to it.

From Action to Passion

A central theme in the story of Jesus's arrest is being "handed over." In the Garden of Gethsemane, Jesus was handed over to Roman authorities. Some translations say he was "betrayed," but the Greek says that Jesus was "handed over" by Judas (see Mark 14:10). The same word is used not only for Judas but also for God. "Jesus was handed over for our sins" (Rom. 4:25). "God did not spare Jesus, but handed him over to benefit us all" (Rom. 8:32). So this term, *handed over,* is important in the spiritual movement from action to passion.

The drama of being handed over radically divides the life of Jesus in two parts. The first part of his life is filled with activity and initiative. Jesus speaks; he preaches; he heals; he travels. But immediately after he is handed over, Jesus becomes the one to whom things are done. He is arrested; he is led to the high priest; he's taken before Pilate; he's crowned with thorns; he's nailed on a cross. Things are being done to him over which he has no control.

This is the meaning of *passion* ("to suffer")—being the recipient of other people's actions. It is important for us to realize that when Jesus says, "It is accomplished" (John 19:30), he does not simply mean, "I have done all the things I wanted to do." He also means, "I have allowed things to be done to me that needed to be done to me to fulfill my vocation." Jesus fulfills his vocation not in action only, but also in passion.

We are preoccupied in our culture with staying in control. Our self-esteem is largely based on our ability to stay active, take the initiative, and set directions for our lives. We consider the active life a sign of being fully human ("Yes, he/she is still very active"). The reality is that we have very little control over our lives. Most things are done to us or not determined by us (the color of our skin, our nationality, social status, family of origin, education, and so on). And our common destination is death. At certain times we can hide our lack of control better than at other times, but more often we have no choice but to let other people, circumstances, and events determine much of our life direction. The challenge is to see our passion as much as our action as vocation. How are you called to follow the way of Jesus to the cross? How are you called to follow Christ to new life? Both are parts of following Jesus in life and in death.

After I joined Daybreak as a man in my fifties, I began to see how much I lived in the illusion of control. As I entered more fully into the community, I began to learn from those in the community who had little or no say about what they ate or wore, or what they did or where they went. I began to think more about my own life and how little is determined by what I think, say, or do. I am inclined to protest this and prefer all to be action, originated by me as master of my fate. But the truth is that my suffering for love is a much greater part of my life than my action. Not to recognize this is self-deception, and not to embrace my passion with love is self-rejection. Therefore it becomes increasingly important to recognize that our vocation is fulfilled not just in our actions but also in passion.

Passion is a kind of waiting—waiting for what other people are going to do. All action ends in passion. To love another is to realize that they have the power and freedom to hand us over to suffering, whether intentionally or not. When we are handed over, we wait to be acted upon. When the time comes, we let go of our wishes and desires and wait open-endedly for others to act, for God to deliver, giving up control over our future and letting God define our lives.

These insights into the passion of Jesus were very important in the discussions with my friend suffering from cancer. He realized that after much hard work he had to wait. He came to see that his vocation as a human being would be fulfilled not just in his actions but also in his passion. And together we began to understand that precisely in this waiting, some new hope, new peace, and even new joy would gradually emerge.

From Leading to Being Led

After nearly twenty years in the academic world, I began to sense a restlessness and saw it as a new call to vocation, which led me to Daybreak. At this time, I was entering my fifties, unlikely to ever double my years, and I came face-to-face with a simple question: Did becoming older bring me closer to Jesus?

Somehow I had come to believe that growing older and more mature meant that I would be increasingly able to offer leadership. In fact, I had grown more self-confident over the years. I felt I knew something and had the ability to express it well and be heard. In that sense, I felt more and more in control. Yet I found myself praying poorly, living somewhat isolated from other people, and becoming very much preoccupied with burning issues. Everyone was saying that I was doing really well, but something inside was telling me that my success was putting my own soul in danger. In the midst of this crisis, I kept praying: "Lord, show me where you want me to go and I will follow you, but please be clear and unambiguous about it!" Well, God was clear, even though it took me a long time to discern that I was to live among the poor in spirit for my own healing as well as theirs.

My move from Harvard to L'Arche—from the "best and the brightest," who wanted to rule the world, to men and women who had few or no words that could be heard by our society—felt like a move from leading to being led. After twenty-five years of priesthood, being free to go where I wanted and doing what I chose, I found my place in a small, hidden life with people whose broken minds and bodies demanded a strict daily routine.

When I joined the community, my independent ways were challenged. I came to realize that every hour, day, and month were full of surprises—often surprises I was least prepared for. When Bill, one of my friends and core members, agreed or disagreed with my sermons, he did not wait until after Mass to tell me so! He might tell me right in the middle of the service. Logical ideas did not receive logical responses. Present feelings and deep emotions could no longer be held in check by beautiful words and convincing arguments. Without realizing it, the people I came to live with made me aware of the extent to which my leadership was still based in a desire to control complex situations, confused emotions, and anxious minds. It took me a long time to feel safe in this unpredictable climate. L'Arche offered me God's solution to my burnout and put me in touch with the mystery that vocation and leadership, for a large part, means to be led into the realities of relationship and the challenges of love.[7]

To know God's will, I have to listen to his voice, become obedient when he calls, and follow wherever he leads. Even when I do not like it, even when it is not a place of comfort or satisfaction and he demands that I go where I might not have chosen to go.

Jesus learned obedience from his suffering (Heb. 5:7–9). This means that his pains and struggles made him able to listen more perfectly to God. In and through his sufferings, he came to know God's heart and could respond to his call. For me, entering into the suffering of the poor is a way to become obedient—that is, a listener to God. Suffering accepted and shared in love breaks down my selfish defenses and sets me free to accept God's guidance.

Jesus's Challenge to Peter

I have gone back again and again to the story of Jesus and Peter after the resurrection. After commissioning him three times to "feed my sheep," Jesus said to Peter:

> In all truth I tell you. When you were young you put on your own belt and walked where you liked; but when you grow old you will stretch out your hands and somebody else will put a belt round you and take you where you would rather not go. (John 21:18)

Jesus's profound words to Peter touch the core of Christian obedience and offer us ever new ways to let go of power and follow the humble way of Jesus. The world says, "When you were young, you were dependent and could not go where you wanted, but when you grow old, you will be able to make your own decisions, go your own way, and control your own destiny." But Jesus has a different vision of maturity: it is the ability and willingness to be led where you would rather not go.

My movement from Harvard to L'Arche made me aware of how much my own thinking had been affected by the desire to be relevant, popular, and powerful. The truth, however, is that these are not vocations but temptations. Jesus asks, "Do you love me?" Jesus sends us out to be shepherds, and Jesus promises a life in which we increasingly have to stretch out our hands and be led to places where we would rather not go. He asks us to move from a concern for relevance to a life of prayer, from worries about popularity to communal and mutual ministry, and from a leadership built on power to a leadership in which we critically discern where God is leading us.

Since my vocation, like Peter's, is to be led to where Jesus wants me to "feed [his] sheep," I have to be willing to lay down my life for them (see John 10:11). This might in special circumstances mean dying for others, but it means first of all making our own lives—our sorrows and joys, our despair and hope, our loneliness and experience of intimacy—available to others as sources of new life. One of the greatest gifts we can give to others is ourselves. We offer consolation and comfort, especially in moments of crisis, when we say, "Do not be afraid, I know what you are living and I am living it with you. You are not alone." Thus, we become Christlike shepherds.

The challenge to Peter reminds us that Jesus's transition from action to passion must also be ours if we want to follow his way. We, too, have to let ourselves be "handed over" and thus fulfill our vocation.

As we grow older or more spiritually mature, we, too, may be handed over, and with outstretched hands be guided and led to places we would rather not go. What was true for Peter will be true for us. Suffering is ahead. A hard obedience. We will be tempted to think we have chosen the wrong road. But instead of being surprised by the pain, be surprised by the joy in obedience. Be surprised by the immense healing power that keeps bursting forth like springs from the depth of our pain. Be surprised by the little flower that shows its beauty in the midst of a barren desert.

My friend Jean-Louis was surprised by how much he had changed after returning from Calcutta, where he had lived with the L'Arche community and worked in one of Mother Teresa's homes for the dying. He told me, "When I returned home, I felt grateful, strong, and ready to continue my work. But then, a few days later, it suddenly happened. I have few words for it. It was not culture shock, or a sudden realization of what I had seen, nor a simple re-entry crisis. But something much deeper. I suddenly realized that I had seen God in Calcutta and that I was a different person because of it. It felt like an invitation to surrender, to let go, to completely trust, to be remolded by love."

As Jean-Louis tried to find words for his experience of being led, I wanted to weep with him, not tears of sadness but of joy. It was joy that the "old person" who wants to plan, organize, control, do things, and plan the future was gradually dying, and the "new person," who is completely malleable in the Potter's hands, was being born. Somewhere within I felt a certain jealousy. I wanted to be as open, flexible, and ready for the Spirit to lead as Jean-Louis was, but my main emotion was simply gratitude to see a friend so deeply blessed.

The Practice of Theological Reflection

My friend learned to live with openness to be led by the Spirit without the need to control his future. He had learned to surrender to the movement of God. What, then, is the spiritual discipline required to live with outstretched hands? My friend learned surrender by living with the very poor and reflecting on his life in light of God's call. I propose that the practice of strenuous theological reflection allows us to discern critically where we are being led. Real theological reflection is thinking with the "mind of Christ" (1 Cor. 2:16); it is reflecting on the painful and joyful realities of each day with the mind of Jesus, thereby raising human consciousness to the knowledge of God's gentle guidance. This is hard discipline, since God's presence is often a hidden presence that needs to be discovered.

In thinking about the future of Christian leadership, I am convinced that it needs to be a theological leadership. For this to happen, change has to happen in seminaries and divinity schools and Christian communities. We need centers where people are trained in true discernment of the signs of the times. They cannot offer just an intellectual training. Deep spiritual formation is required, involving the whole person—body, mind, and heart. Formation in the mind of Christ, "who did not cling to power but emptied himself, taking the form of a slave, who did not cling" (Phil. 2:6-8) is not what most seminaries are about. But to the degree that such formation is being sought after and realized, there is hope for the church of the twenty-first century. The oldest, most traditional vision of Christian leadership is still a vision that awaits its realization in the future.

Servant Christian leaders, then, practice solid theological reflection, know the heart of God, and are equipped—through prayer, study, and careful analysis—to manifest God's saving work in the midst of the seemingly random events of their time. They can think, speak, and act in the name of Jesus. They are able to discern from moment to moment how God acts in human history and how the personal, communal, national, and international events that occur during our lives can make us more sensitive to the ways we are led to the cross and through the cross to the resurrection.

Jesus came in the fullness of time. He will come again in the fullness of time. Wherever the Christ is, time is brought to its fullness. Our spiritual task is to "seize the time"—the right time for God's purpose here and now.

All the great events of the gospels occur in the fullness of *time* (as a literal translation of the Greek word *kairos* shows clearly): "When the *time* for Elizabeth had *become full* she bore her son John" (Luke 1:57). "The time has come to its fullness and the kingdom of God is close at hand" (Mark 1:15). "When the *time had come to completion*, God sent his Son, born of a woman" (Gal. 4:4), and in the fullness of time God will "bring everything together under Christ, as head, everything in the heavens and everything on earth" (Eph. 1:10).

It is in the fullness of time that we meet God and know what we are called to be and do.

EXERCISES FOR DEEPER DISCERNMENT

1. *Kairos* time is the fullness of God's presence, and chronological time is marked by predictable periods. What does it mean to you to act according to *kairos* time? Is this an easy or difficult concept for you? Can you recall a time when you acted when "time was full"? Describe it.

2. Waiting with patience, being "handed over" to go where you don't want to be led, entering into the passion and suffering of life are all named in this chapter as part of spiritual maturity. Does this match your own experience? Is there an example you can share with your small group?

3. Nouwen's friend returned from Calcutta saying his time there "felt like an invitation to surrender, to let go, to completely trust, to be remolded by love." Do you believe that suffering and living close to vulnerability offers an "invitation to surrender"? Is this a romantic notion of suffering or a realistic one?

4. How are you called to follow the way of Jesus to the cross? How are you called to follow Christ to new life? Write about these two aspects of discipleship. How do they intersect in your life?

5. This book started with a definition: "Discernment is a type of faithful living and listening that ascertains and affirms the unique way God's love and direction are manifested so that we can know God's will and fulfill our individual calling and shared mission." How have you learned to live and listen faithfully to better discern God's activity in your life? List several specific ways you will continue to discern your vocation and direction.

Discerning the Hidden Wholeness

I am a member of the L'Arche community, Daybreak, in Toronto—part of a worldwide network of communities where people with physical and intellectual disabilities and their assistants live together in the spirit of the Beatitudes. It was founded in 1964 by the Canadian Jean Vanier and the French Dominican Thomas Philippe, in the little village of Trosly-Breuil. Although the original members of the community were Roman Catholic, soon new communities were started in which Protestants of various denominations, together with Roman Catholics and Jews, started sharing their lives and ministry. When L'Arche was welcomed into India, Muslims and Hindus also became part of the L'Arche family. Today, L'Arche is an interreligious faith community broadly defined as seeking to discern what Thomas Merton called a "deep ecumenism" and a "hidden wholenesss" beneath the surface of obvious differences.

Recognizing the reality and presence of Christ in our midst is an ongoing process of discernment in which members participate to varying degrees. For me as a resident priest and pastor at L'Arche, it is an experience of and participation in what the church calls the "communion of saints."

I've also seen how God speaks to me through the poor. They teach me that being is more important than doing, the heart is more important than the mind, and doing things together is more important than doing things alone. Discernment is a way of recognizing that God is not limited by our conception of who belongs to him and who does not, or who is right and who is wrong. For as the scripture says, "In [God] we live and move and have our being" (Acts 17:28 NRSV). The mystery of discernment is that "deep calls to deep" and heart speaks to heart.

Those who have received the "mind of Christ" deep in their hearts can discern the presence of Christ in all persons and in all things. The place where Jesus's heart and our hearts intersect is the hidden wholeness of the body of Christ. It is not some reality to be accomplished in the future, but a gift already present, here and now, even when not fully visible. With the eyes of faith, we can gradually discern this already present unity made manifest in our particular communities of faith.

This essential wholeness is evident in very practical ways whenever people of good will from different faith traditions come together in a spirit of unity to really listen to one another, pray or meditate together, study scripture in small groups, share our traditions, and discover each other's gifts. And while it seems impossible for Christians from different denominations, and people from different faith traditions, to participate in the same Eucharist, there remains the deeper reality that the celebration of Word and Sacrament is anchored in the wholeness that one day will take a more visible form.

It is my conviction that something new is being born here, and that it will transform the face of the churches and communities of faith in the centuries to come. The gift of wholeness is already most dramatically revealed through the lives of the poor. Where the poor are found, there is Christ. In the words of the Taizé chant, *"Ubi caritas, et amor, ubi caritas Deus ibi est"*—"Where there is charity and love, God is there!"

Through our common concern for the poor, many people who seemed far apart in doctrinal formulations, liturgical styles, and spiritual practices find themselves living and working together in unity; they are able to move their attention away from what otherwise divides them. The good news for the church is that, whenever we direct our attention to the poor, we find the wholeness of the body of Christ.

The practical questions remain: How do we live out our common life as a God-centered, love-motivated community of faith? How will we express our particular faith in prayers and worship that include all people? How will we live our unity in authentic ways, fully recognizing the divisions and separations that continue to exist among us? My own growing awareness is that spiritual needs and desires are present and common to all, that we share a universal quest for deeper meaning and purpose, and that we are all beloved children of God.

I see our community moving toward the practice of several simple principles of spiritual unity: 1) we recognize the presence of God in the poor as the centerpiece of worship, 2) we affirm the differences and uniqueness of each tradition present, 3) we come together regularly for prayer and meditation, 4) we find ways to celebrate the Word and Sacrament, and, 5) we live the spiritual life in ordinary, everyday ways. Together, these are the portals to unity and for discerning the divine presence among us. The key to success is to see ourselves as servants of God and to each other. "I am your servant, O God, grant me discernment that I may understand your ways" (Ps. 119:125).

APPENDIX A

We Drink from Our Own Wells: Discernment and Liberation

by Henri Nouwen

"Everyone has to drink from his own well," observed Saint Bernard of Clairvaux. Yet no one drinks alone. We all have drunk from wells we did not dig and enjoyed fresh water that is not entirely our own.

According to Gustavo Gutiérrez, the father of Liberation Theology, "Spirituality is like living water that springs up in the very depths of the experience of faith."[1] To drink from your own well is to live your own life in the Spirit of Jesus as you have encountered him in your concrete historical reality. This has nothing to do with abstract opinions, convictions, or ideas, but it has everything to do with the tangible, audible, and visible experience of God. As the First Epistle of John puts it: "What we have heard, what we have seen with our eyes, what we have looked upon and our hands have touched—this we proclaim as the word of life" (1 John 1:1).

By dipping deeply into the well of our own lives, we can discern the movements of God's Spirit in our lives. Careful discernment remains our lifelong task. I can see no other way for discernment than a life in the Spirit, a life of unceasing prayer and contemplation, a life of deep communion with the Spirit of God. Such a life will slowly develop in us an inner sensitivity, enabling us to distinguish between the law of the flesh and the law of the Spirit. We certainly will make constant errors and seldom have the purity of heart required to make the right decisions all the time. But when we continually try to live in the Spirit, we at least will be willing to confess our weakness and limitations in all humility, trusting in the one who is greater than our hearts.

At the same time, we practice our discernment not alone but in community.

The question is not simply, "Where does God lead me as an individual person who tries to do his will?" More basic and more significant is the question, "Where does God lead us as a people?" This question requires that we pay careful attention to God's guidance in our life together, and that together we search for a creative response to the way we have heard God's voice in our midst.

Likewise, spiritual discernment is based on a concrete and dynamic spirituality that demands constant, careful listening to the people of God, especially the poor. It does not allow for a fixed and definite theory that can be applied at all times and in all places. It requires great attentiveness to the continually new movements of the Spirit among the children of God. That in turn requires an ear that has been well trained by the scriptures and the church's understanding of those scriptures. A constant dialogue is necessary between the "old knowing" of scripture and tradition and the "new knowing" of the concrete, daily life experiences of the people of God.

I remember a summer course I attended in Lima, Peru, in 1982, where Gustavo first presented the main themes of his spirituality of liberation. This course was one of the most significant experiences of my six-month stay in Latin America. I was part of an unusual learning event in which approximately two thousand community workers and "pastoral agents" from many countries participated. These young men and women had lived the Latin American reality, had encountered the Lord, and had drunk deeply from the "fountains of living water" flowing from their hearts (John 7:38). Most of them were born and raised in poor barrios and had become activists in their communities of liberation. They knew their own people and had learned to think with one eye on the gospel and one eye on the painful reality they shared with the people. They worked in their various districts and countries as catechists, social workers, or project coordinators. They were all deeply immersed in the Bible and had come to think of themselves as people of God called to the Promised Land.

As one who has been exposed to many styles of theological liberalism in the North, I was struck by the orthodoxy of this Christ-centered spirituality in the Southern Hemisphere. The Christians of Latin America, Gustavo himself pointed out to me, came to a realization of the social dimension of their faith without going through a modernistic phase. For example, Archbishop Oscar Romero, that traditional churchman, in his direct contact with the suffering people of El Salvador, became a social critic without ever rejecting, or even criticizing, his traditional past. His biblical understanding of God's presence in history and in the community of faith was the basis and source of his courageous protest against the exploitation and oppression of the people, a protest that led to his martyrdom.

Talking with Father Gutiérrez and his students that summer made me aware of how individualistic and elitist my own spirituality had been. In many respects my thinking about the spiritual life had been deeply influenced by my North American milieu, with its emphasis on the interior life and the methods and techniques for developing that life. Only when I confronted what Gustavo calls the "irruption of the poor into history" did I become aware of how "spiritualized" my spirituality had become. It had been, in fact, a spirituality for introspective persons who have the luxury of the time and space needed to develop inner harmony and quietude. Gustavo's spirituality of liberation does not allow for such reductionism.[2]

What I learned from Gustavo was that liberating spirituality must be rooted in an active and reflective faith, not a passive, private, or privileged contemplative experience. And that spiritual discernment is not just an individual gift but part of the struggle of the people of God. That's what he means when he says, "We must drink from our own wells."[3]

Although I live with and minister with people with physical and intellectual disabilities, my travels and mission trips to other countries have revealed to me another type of handicap: the disability of nations stemming from a broken history, centuries of oppression and exploitation, the neglect and indifference of wealthier nations, and social sins of injustice, war, and greed. Not only are individuals poor, disabled, or marginalized in our world, but entire countries (both people and social structures) are poor and oppressed and in need of compassion and transformation. In the end we will be judged by how we treat both individuals and nations (see Matt. 25).

By recognizing the divine presence in the midst of the struggle, we can discern that the struggle has already been won. We already possess that for which we strive. We already taste that for which we hunger. We simply aim to make fully visible a victory that has been accomplished. This reality makes possible a community life characterized by true love, joy, and peace and revealed in Jesus, who invites us to "come and see" what God has done and continues to do in our midst.

"Following the footsteps of Jesus," says Gustavo, without departing from the real world and "paths of solidarity with society's marginalized and insignificant" is the tension required in discerning God's will for humanity and Christ's call to action in this world. What he calls the "interruption of the poor"—their presence and place in history—is a genuine irruption of God in the world. And our physical encounter with God's poor is a spiritual encounter with Christ himself. As Gustavo writes, "This God who pitches his tent among us, questions us. That irruption is the source of our spirituality—our journey toward God."

APPENDIX B

Henri Nouwen on
Hearing a Deeper Beat

by Michael J. Christensen

Let each step to the music which he hears, however
measured or far away.

—Henry David Thoreau

For Henri Nouwen, *discernment* is both a spiritual gift and a
practice that "ascertains and affirms the unique way God's love
and direction are manifested in our lives, so that we can know
God's will and fulfill our calling and mission within the mysterious interworkings of God's love."[1] His use of the word is based
on the biblical notion of "discernment of spirits" as a gift of the

Spirit (1 Cor. 12:10), rooted in the core disciplines of the Christian life—prayer, community, worship, and ministry—which leads to a life "worthy of our calling" (Col. 1:10). As Robert Jonas put it in the foreword, discernment is an inner "listening and responding to that place within us where our deepest desires align with God's desire." I would add to the definition of discernment, *spiritual understanding and intuitive perception found in solitude and community, through which we can situate ourselves in time and space to know God's will and do God's work in the world.*

In chapter 1 of this volume, Nouwen describes discernment as "hearing a deeper sound" beneath the noise of ordinary life, and "seeing through" appearances to the *interconnectedness* of all things, to gain a vision of "how things hang together" (*theoria physike*) in our lives and in the world. The metaphor of *hearing a deeper sound or beat* is what I want to explore in this brief reflection—specifically, how he hears and reads the signs of daily life. While there are many methods and approaches, Nouwen's method of discernment can be summarized as follows: 1) stop and listen to the beat, 2) march to the music you hear, 3) order your steps with the saints, and 4) read the signs along the way.

STOP AND LISTEN TO THE BEAT

There's something primordial about a drumbeat. Spiritual discernment, Henri Nouwen writes, means "to listen to God, to pay attention to God's active presence. . . . When we are truly listening, we come to know that God is speaking to us, pointing the way, showing the direction. We simply need to learn to keep our ears open. Discernment is a life of listening to a deeper sound and marching to a different beat, a life in which we become 'all ears'" (chapter 1). In Berkeley, where I live, there's a local church called The Table that hosts a monthly drumming circle that meets in a tutoring center. The circle has a leader who starts the beat, and the rest of us join in with a rhythm we have been learning. But soon, we are playing off each other's movements, in sync with a deeper beat, until the group as a whole gradually slows to a halt. By getting in touch with our own inner drummer, so to speak, we find resonance with each other and with a hidden drummer.[2]

Henri Nouwen appropriated the drumming metaphor for spiritual discernment in 1974, when he was on retreat at the Trappist Abbey of the Genesee in upstate New York. There in the quiet monastery he saw a reproduction of Hazard Durfee's painting of a flute player with a now familiar quote by Henry David Thoreau: "Why should we be in such desperate haste to succeed, and in such desperate enterprises? If a man does not keep pace with his companions, perhaps it is because he hears a different drummer. Let him step to the music which he hears, however measured or far away" (*Walden*, chapter 8).[3]

The deeper wisdom of Thoreau, as well as Emerson and other transcendentalists, points to the possibility of breaking cadence with conventional thinking (what the Bible calls the "spirit of the world"), listening to a different beat (intuition), and stepping to the music you hear (courage). Let's extend this metaphor of spiritual discernment.

MARCH TO THE MUSIC YOU HEAR

Once you hear the beat of a different drummer, you can march to the music you hear. Consider the composition of the Psalms. What kind of music did the psalmist hear when he composed the lines of Psalm 146?

> Praise the LORD! Praise the LORD, O my soul!
>   I will praise the LORD as long as I live; I will sing praises
> to my God all my life long.

Do not put your trust in princes, in mortals, in whom there is no help. When their breath departs, they return to the earth; on that very day their plans perish.

Happy are those whose help is the God of Jacob, whose hope is in the LORD their God, who made heaven and earth, the sea, and all that is in them; who keeps faith forever;

The LORD executes justice for the oppressed; he gives food to the hungry. The LORD sets the prisoners free; the LORD opens the eyes of the blind.

The LORD lifts up those who are bowed down; the LORD loves the righteous.

The LORD watches over the strangers; he upholds the orphan and the widow, but the way of the wicked he brings to ruin.

Many psalms in the Hebrew Bible are traditionally attributed to the shepherd boy David, who heard God sing and played God's songs on his harp. When we hear and chant a psalm like this one—which goes so counter to how we often think about the poor—are we not harmonizing with the voice of the living God? Expanding the musical metaphor, I suggest that the maker of heaven and earth and all the fish in the sea can be conceived as a master musician or a heavenly harpist or a different drummer. As such, the Lord God, and those in tune with God, play songs of justice for the poor, food for the hungry, freedom for the captive, sight for the blind, protection for the stranger, and care for the orphan and widow. Such songs bring down the proud and lift up the humble.

Spiritual discernment requires us to put our ears to ground that we may hear the low notes that vibrate for the poor and keep us focused on what is most important—that is, whom God cares most about. Once we hear and heed that deeper sound, we can march to the music we may only faintly hear, however measured or far away. But what if we miss a step, a beat, a note or two?

Stop and listen again. . . . "Whether you turn to the right or to the left, your ears will hear a voice behind you, saying, 'This is the way; walk in it'" (Isa. 30:21 NIV). In other words, when you come to a fork in your road, you will hear a voice behind you—what Nouwen calls the "inner voice of love"—that reminds you of God's presence and reveals to you God's will, sometimes specifically which way to turn.

Order My Steps

"Order my steps in the Word," gospel choirs often sing.[4] This anthem is based on Proverbs 20:24 (from the compilation of wise sayings sponsored by King Solomon). The proverb says simply, "All our steps are ordered by the Lord; how then can we understand our own ways?" We cannot, of course, fully understand the ways of God, or even our own ways; we simply cast ourselves into the loving hands of the living God, who alone knows and understands the steps we take. As Henri Nouwen says, "You can't see the whole path ahead, but there is usually enough light to take the next step." And then to trust God's guidance in the moment.

In terms of "ordering our steps in the Word," Nouwen recommends the practice of *lectio divina,* spiritual reading. What shimmers and resonates for you when you read a text devotionally? "*Lectio divina* means to read the Bible with reverence and openness to what the Spirit is saying to us in the present moment. When we approach the Word of God (*logos*) as a word spoken to me (*rhema*), God's presence and will can be made known."[5]

Nouwen would also add that it is important to "order my steps with the saints." Certainly the Bible helps us order our steps, but we also have the saints (both the living and the dead) in our lives to help us hear and walk in the way of the Lord. Thus we are not alone in stepping out in faith: "Therefore, since we are surrounded by such a great cloud of witnesses, let us throw off everything that hinders and the sin that so easily entangles. And let us run with perseverance the race marked out for us, fixing our eyes on Jesus, the pioneer and perfecter of faith. For the joy set before him he endured the cross, scorning its shame, and sat down at the right hand of the throne of God" (Hebrews 12:1–2 NIV). If God orders my steps, Nouwen would say, then it's not just me alone deciding what steps to take. We are all part of the body of Christ, the community of faith, and we do not act alone. As part of the church universal, we are connected to others in the body of Christ—past, present, and future. The entire communion of saints is available to us as we order our steps on the journey of faith, as Nouwen says in chapter 5 of this book:

> Although we tend to think of saints as holy and pious, picturing them with halos above their heads and ecstatic gazes, true saints are much more accessible. Whether they are still living or have joined the "great cloud of witnesses," they are available to help us in time of need. . . . Beyond the strength I received from friends who remembered to pray for me during a fearful time, I also have experienced a special closeness to certain saints or holy ones in the church's memory who speak to me of faithful witness and strength, sometimes providing guidance in time of need. In times of struggle, I do not hesitate to ask them to pray for me, as they encourage me to practice discernment and live a spiritual life.

READ THE SIGNS

There are many kinds of signs: road signs, commercial signs, for sale signs, biblical signs and wonders, and signs of the times in current events, as well as spiritual signs for decision making, confirmation, where to go next, what to do with your life, and how to treat your neighbor. Nouwen shows us how to read the signs of daily life for the purpose of discernment.

One of the courses I teach at Drew University is on C. S. Lewis and J. R. R. Tolkien, who shared a common interest in semiotics—interpreting signs. For these writers, at least in their fiction, learning how to read the signs is a matter of life and death. For example, in Lewis's *Chronicles of Narnia*, Aslan instructs young Jill Pole to read and remember the signs on which her life depends: "But, first, remember, remember, remember the signs. Say them to yourself when you wake in the morning and when you lie down at night, and when you wake in the middle of the night. And whatever strange things may happen to you, let nothing turn your mind from following the signs."[6]

Signs embody and point beyond themselves to hidden meaning and purpose beneath the surface of mere appearances. Signs are there on our road of life to call our attention, confirming or challenging the way we are going. Of course, there are countless signs out there just waiting to be interpreted, and you cannot build your faith on "signs and wonders." Spiritually, however, at least according to Nouwen, we can pray to God to confirm or challenge our inclinations by showing us signs.[7] For example, a friend of mine, Jeff Markay, told me that when he asked Henri Nouwen for spiritual advice in making a vocational decision, Nouwen responded in his thick Dutch accent: "Pray this prayer: 'Lord, make it clear, make it really, really clear.'"

Nouwen believed that God speaks to us all the time and in many ways: through dreams and imagination, friends and people you meet, good books and great ideas, nature's beauty, and critical and current events. But it requires spiritual discernment to hear God's voice, see what God sees, and read the signs of daily life.[8] What he learned from his mentor, Thomas Merton, and passes on in this volume is how to read the signs of God's guidance in *books, nature, people,* and *events.*

The place to begin to look for God's guidance, Nouwen suggests, is in what we are drawn to read—spiritual reading, not only the Bible but good books and human literature that are lifted beyond themselves by the Spirit to become vehicles of divine communication. This also includes the Book of Nature. The signs of God's presence in creation—trees and flowers, sun and stars, snow and rain, and more—remind us that God's first language is nature and God calls us to love and cherish the good creation.

God also speaks to us "through the people who speak to us about the things of God," as Nouwen writes in chapter 5. People with whom we have a primary, intimate, or intensive relationship, he says, are human vehicles of divine presence and direction. They often plant seeds and prepare the way for a future not yet revealed. From a spiritual perspective, certain people are in our lives for a season, or a reason, or a lifetime. One of the ways the Spirit guides and shapes our lives is through those we find on our path. When we receive those placed in our lives as gifts of God, they become living signs pointing the way to God, home, vocation, or a new direction.

Beyond showing how *books, nature,* and *people* can be interpreted as signs pointing to God's wisdom and guidance, Nouwen adds *events* to the list of daily signs. He learned from Merton that certain *events*—current events, historical events, critical incidents, and life circumstances—can serve as signposts pointing to the will of God for those with "eyes to see and ears to hear." Spiritual lessons can be learned from what occurred in the past, revealing new truths and insights in historical events. In every critical event, says Nouwen, "there is an opportunity for God to act creatively, and reveal a deeper truth than what we can see on the surface of things."[9] God also speaks to us in the circumstances and seemingly random events of our lives, giving our lives more meaning. Discernment is the spiritual art of recognizing God in the many events, meetings, and situations we experience in daily life.

Beyond the five senses and the faculty of reaso
its own ways of hearing, seeing, and knowing.
the right side of our brains, or perhaps deep witl
the human soul, there is a spiritual organ that c
hear the beat, step to the music, and read the signs. God seldom
speaks directly or face-to-face. Instead, God speaks in whispers,
signs, and symbols, in a still, small voice that requires theological
reflection and spiritual interpretation.

The messages we find in books, nature, people, and events
form the context for discernment. Through prayerful reflection
and community support, we are led to make decisions, commit
to actions, and receive confirmations of what we hope and trust
may be God's will. "In the final analysis," Nouwen concludes, "all
we have are signs that lead us to *suspect* something unspeakably
great":

"[As] it is written: 'What no eye has seen, what no ear has
heard, and what no human mind has conceived'—the things God
has prepared for those who love him—these are the things God
has revealed to us by his Spirit. The Spirit searches all things,
even the deep things of God" (1 Cor. 2:9–10 NIV).[10]

APPENDIX C

Spiritual Friendship and Mutual Discernment

by Robert A. Jonas

In early summer 1985, I sat beside my fiancée, Margaret, in the stern of a thirty-foot sailboat as we plowed through seven-foot seas off the Atlantic coast north of Boston. The boat belonged to my soon-to-be father-in-law, John Marshall Bullitt, a retired professor of English at Harvard and an ardent sailor. He was fighting lung cancer, and he knew he probably didn't have long to live. After the three of us had spent an hour at sea, John invited me to take the wheel. He gave me a few basic instructions and sat down across from Margaret. While father and daughter reflected on their shared love of poetry and took turns trying to see which poems they could recite by heart, I kept a grip on the wheel and suppressed a few surges of fear. I had never sailed a boat before. Gusts of wind were pushing the sails from side to side, and from time to time especially large waves threatened to hit us broadside. What if I made a mistake and capsized the boat? I noticed that John would occasionally glance at me and at the sails, but his apparent willingness to focus not on me but on something else had a calming effect. If he trusted me, a total neophyte, to take the helm, maybe I was doing something right. Maybe his instructions plus my own lived experience could teach me what I needed to know about sailing.

I learned a couple of lessons that day not only about sailing but also about discernment. For one thing, I was reminded how much I need and am grateful for helpful guidance. Facing the unknown can be confusing and scary without a mentor; one can become frightened, too shaken to learn much, and make a mess of things. What's more, as I steered us toward a horizon that appeared and disappeared behind the waves, it also occurred to me that sailing, like living, requires our full attention. We may set our goals and have a rough idea of our position, but conditions are always changing, both within us and outside us. To reach our destinations, we must maintain an alert and panoramic awareness as we consider where we want to go and as we assess our ever-changing situation.

As I held the wheel, I kept an eye on the horizon toward which we were headed, though I strained sometimes to locate it amid the tumbling, windswept waves. I was aware of the tilt of the deck, the shifting weight of my body, the height of the waves, the direction, speed, and sound of the gusty winds, the distance and orientation of the horizon, and the sight and sound of the mainsail and jib. Glancing at the compass, I discovered that I could not keep our direction steadily on course every moment. Because of the dynamic environment, I had to do what sailors call "tacking." I had to weave my way toward that horizon, which periodically disappeared. Just like life, I thought: momentarily

I lose my way, study the compass, and look for the big red *N* on the dial, recalibrating my course and readjusting my hands on the wheel. In the midst of the changes and challenges of life, how easy it is to forget who we are, why we are here, and where we think we are going.

Every religion, every spiritual path, and every secular self-improvement program offers its followers a conceptual map of the journey, providing a destination and some structure and guidelines for how to reach it. Discernment has been an important topic of Christian reflection for over two thousand years, and each denomination or sect takes a slightly different approach. The goal or destination of Christian living may sound straightforward: to be a follower of Jesus Christ. But what does that mean, and how does one determine whether one is truly living a Christian life? What does God desire from me and for me? How do I know if I am doing God's will?

Some Christians emphasize the moral dimension of discipleship—that is, learning to behave according to the values and ethical principles that Jesus espoused, primarily to love God and neighbor, including one's enemies, with a focus on what actions we do or do not take. Other Christians emphasize the subjective dimension of discernment, focusing less on external behavior and more on interior feelings, thoughts, intentions, and overall awareness throughout the day. Of course, both subjective experience and objective behavior are important, and here, too, the metaphor of tacking is helpful. As we discern our way, we move our attention between inner and outer experience, adjusting and correcting our course as needed.

For Christians who highlight morality and behavior, discernment involves a daily appraisal of one's actions. At the end of the day, one might ask oneself: Did I treat others kindly today? Did I support the cause of justice in concrete ways? Did I help the poor? Did I do what Jesus might have done in this situation? What is God calling me to do now?

Ideally, this assessment or discernment is carried out not just in solitude but also in relationship. For Christians it is important to be accountable to a larger community—one's faith community, for instance, and one's family or household. Scripture encourages us to tell the truth in love when we perceive that other people's behavior is damaging them or others. And Jesus's stories and teachings urge us to ask ourselves (and sometimes other people) whether we are behaving in loving and empathic ways, and whether we are willing to change our selfish or destructive behaviors in response to what we learn.

For Christians who practice discernment with an emphasis on subjective experience, discernment evokes questions that focus on the inner flow of experience. As I look back over the day, how and where did I sense the presence of God? How did I respond? What did I feel in the course of the day, and how did I share it with God? Did my thoughts dwell on judging a particular person or reliving bitterness about a past slight? Did I imagine violating a trust or telling even a little white lie? Did I notice moments of the peace that Jesus promises—the inner peace that lies shimmering beneath our worry, opinions, and preoccupations? What is God inviting me to see and hear?

Subjective discernment requires continuous attention to the flow of memories, images, thoughts, emotions, and sensations within us. It is never over and done with. Our feelings and motives are fickle, so Christians need disciplines of prayer, meditation, and contemplation that focus our attention and give us strength and courage to keep heading toward our sacred destination in the midst of uncertain and often volatile weather.

As long as we live, we are at sea, in motion, heading toward home as we tack through the waves with the boat, the companions, and the weather that we have been given. It is cause for joy when a guide comes along who can help us discern our way.

HENRI NOUWEN, MASTER SAILOR

Father Henri Nouwen was an extraordinary sailor on the high seas of the inward way. I met Henri in 1983, at a tumultuous time of my life. My marriage was falling apart, and my self-esteem was at low ebb. A doctoral student in psychology and education at Harvard University, I was working three jobs and felt anxious and without direction. I loved my course work but had no clear idea what my vocation was. Several fellow students told me about a new professor at Harvard Divinity School, a preacher, retreat leader, and prolific writer of spiritual books who seemed to possess a kind of spiritual fire, a capacity to inspire people to connect with God. When I heard that Henri Nouwen would give an evening talk at Saint Paul's Church in Harvard Square, I resolved to go.

As I walked into the undercroft where Henri would speak, I was doubtful about continuing my Christian journey. I had been raised a Lutheran and, as a Dartmouth undergraduate, had turned to Taoist and Buddhist meditation. After graduating in 1969, I navigated my spiritual journey with the guidance of books by Thomas Merton, the Trappist monk who understood the depths of contemplative practice and who explored the connections between Buddhist and Christian understandings of ultimate reality. In 1975, I converted to Roman Catholicism and took vows as a Third Order Carmelite, a layperson associated with the Common monastery in Peterborough, New Hampshire.

While working as an organic farmer, I regularly attended Mass at the monastery, and I read and prayed with the works of the sixteenth-century Spanish Carmelite saints, John of the Cross and Teresa of Avila. I was convinced that they would resonate with the contemplative, compassionate spirituality that I had found in Buddhism, and with the focus on nature that I treasured in Taoism. I began to appreciate a deep common wellspring of living wisdom that spanned the apparent distance between John of the Cross's "nada" at the top of Mount Carmel and the Buddha's "no self" teaching, between Zen *shunyata* and Christian *kenosis* (the self-emptying of Christ). In the early 1980s I still wanted to be a Christian, but my five years as a graduate student in Cambridge had brought me into contact with some fine teachers of Buddhist meditation, and I had not found a church that seemed right for me.

That night at Saint Paul's Church, Henri Nouwen walked right into the middle of my discernment process, picked up an invisible soul compass that we shared, and pointed to true north. What is your deepest desire, he asked, and where are you headed? Henri had found his answer in Jesus, and as I listened to his stirring talk, I suddenly saw an opening in the fog of confusion that had settled over my heart. It was obvious to me that Jesus was the focus of Henri's spiritual life, and it was instantly clear that I wanted the same certainty about my own path. I realized that I longed to reconnect with my Christian roots.

Hundreds of people had come for Henri's talk that evening, and as he finished answering questions and the applause died down, I suspected that many people were about to line up to speak with him. Before I could think, I walked briskly up to him and asked if he would be my spiritual director. Henri looked a bit surprised, smiled, and said, "I don't know, but let's have lunch in the Square sometime and talk about it." We did have lunch, and then more lunches, and we became fast friends.

Still, our friendship wasn't easy at first. It turned out that each of us was going through an intense process of discernment. Henri was a Dutch priest who held a doctorate in religion and psychology in his homeland, and had studied psychiatry and religion at the Menninger Institute in Kansas. Each year his cardinal in Holland in effect gave him permission to make the whole earth his parish and to go where he felt led. Henri spent most of his time in North America, but when I met him, he did not feel at home at Harvard. In fact, a few years before, Henri had considered giving up the academic life altogether. In the late 1960s he had been a professor at Notre Dame, and in the 1970s, a tenured professor at Yale Divinity School (where Michael Christensen was one of his students). Yet Henri was never comfortable as an academic theologian, and he relinquished tenure at Yale so that he could explore a ministry to peasants in Latin America. Still, it didn't take him long to discover that he missed the intellectual and cultural stimulation of the United States, so Henri eventually accepted a part-time position at Harvard.

In contrast to the work of many Harvard professors, Henri wasn't particularly interested in exploring theories about Jesus and God. He didn't want to talk about God—he wanted to be with God and to introduce students to what he sensed was the pervasive, loving presence of the Holy Spirit that Jesus gives us. Henri searched for ways to bridge the gap between the intellect and the heart, between theological education and liturgy, between thought and devotion. He invented a most unlikely course for Harvard entitled "The Life of the Spirit," and another course that focused on the mystical teachings of the Gospel of John. He invited students to morning Mass and began many of his classes with a contemplative Taizé chant. He was convinced that no matter what sort of work divinity school students eventually pursued, they would receive deep and lasting benefits from cultivating a habit of daily liturgy and prayer.

SEEKING TRUE NORTH

Soon after I met him, Henri confided that he felt longings pulling him in different directions. He wanted to live in community, but he had already tried monastic life and had found that life too lonely. He felt called to be a writer and teacher, but although the academic environment encouraged these vocations, it gave him no satisfying way to be a pastor or to live in community. Where did he belong? This question troubled him, and we explored it at length as our friendship deepened. Our individual discernment processes tacked along together for a while.

Meanwhile I was straddling the worlds of Buddhism and Christianity. Where could I find a community interested in the Buddhist-Christian dialogue? How much time should I devote to my spiritual life, and which practices—Buddhist or Christian—should I take up? In addition, by the mid-1980s I had separated from my first wife and was sharing custody of our daughter, Christine. I was dating Margaret, whom I loved, but I didn't know if I could risk being vulnerable in another marriage. Every day I wondered whether to head for the starboard of single parenting or the port of married life. If I did decide to remarry, should I ask for an annulment of my first marriage, thus staying in the good graces of the Catholic Church? These and other questions blew against me like gusty winds that push a boat hither and yon.

Henri offered me a listening ear and shared his wisdom. His direction to me tended to be spiritual: whatever I decided to do, I should get to know Jesus better through prayer, and I should participate in more retreats.

My advice to Henri was often psychological, for in spite of his spiritual depth, he seemed nervous and driven. I wondered if his anxiety stemmed from his relationship with his mother, who had died a few years earlier, or from his uncertain relationship with his father.

I also wondered if being a gay celibate priest—a sexual orientation that he never disclosed publicly—was an ongoing source of anxiety for him. After all, Henri never wanted to be anything other than a Catholic priest, and yet his own church called gay people "disordered." His gay Catholic friends urged him to "come out," while other friends counseled him to keep his sexual orientation private. Henri was always in the midst of discerning his way through this deeply important question, and he never reached a decision that gave him peace. Though he wanted to bear witness to the validity of being a gay man and a gay priest, he also wanted his ministry to center on Jesus, not on contemporary sexual politics. He was committed to walking with Jesus no matter what—to preaching the gospel and helping people to find meaning in Jesus's life—and he feared that if he revealed publicly that he was gay, his disclosure would inevitably shift people's attention away from Jesus, and the whole focus of his ministry would change. He feared he would no longer be able to function as a priest, and his ministry of proclaiming Jesus would be compromised. Henri wrestled with this dilemma until the day he died.

My thoughts about what he should do wavered from one conversation to the next, for I could see both sides of his predicament. In the end, Henri kept his hands firmly on the wheel of his Jesus ship in the midst of scary crosswinds and never revealed his sexual orientation publicly. Although there were times when I wished he would publicly disclose his sexual orientation, I also respected his complete commitment to the true north of his inner compass. My role was to be a sympathetic listener. Henri's north was set to Jesus, and whatever happened, he trusted that his Jesus would bring him to the eternal presence and peace that he glimpsed in the Eucharist.

For a while, we thought of our relationship as a kind of mutual mentorship. I, with my recent clinical training, was his therapist, and he was my spiritual director. Gradually, however, we discerned that this approach led to unease and competition, so we finally decided to keep it simple and just be friends. Years later, we laughed about this phase of our relationship. Henri was fifteen years older than me; he was famous and I was not. But these differences did not seem to matter much: we enjoyed and trusted each other.

In 1986, Henri found the community that he had been searching for. At Harvard he met a visiting speaker, Jean Vanier, who had established the worldwide L'Arche communities for people with disabilities. Through Jean, Henri was invited to become pastor of a L'Arche community called Daybreak, in Richmond Hill, Ontario.

At about the same time, Margaret and I decided to get married. At first Henri opposed the marriage, saying that I needed an annulment first. But after beginning that process and discovering that some of its requirements violated my conscience, I decided to abandon the quest. Gradually, as Henri and I talked and he got to know Margaret, he saw the grace in our relationship and the wisdom of our marriage, even though it violated his church's teaching. He attended the wedding and blessed our marriage at the reception.

In the late 1980s, Margaret was ordained an Episcopal priest. She invited Henri to preach at the service, but Henri declined, aware that the cardinal in Boston would probably not approve. Instead of giving the sermon, Henri knelt in the reception hall after the service and asked Margaret for a blessing. Here was another movement of deep discernment for Henri, in which he affirmed the ministry of ordained women in the Episcopal Church. It seemed to me that throughout the 1980s and 1990s, Henri's journey of discernment was winding its way toward Jesus and what Jesus's unconditional love requires, even when his own Church was slow to catch up with the way the wind of the Spirit was blowing.

Meanwhile, I was attending Episcopal services, which were a close fit with both my Lutheran and Roman Catholic experiences of liturgy. I could experience the Real Presence in the Eucharist while also forging a new relationship with the Catholic Church. For several years I had trusted the Church as the true north on my inner compass, but when I finally admitted that its views on such issues as the role of women in the Church, contraception, population growth, and sexual orientation contradicted my own moral reasoning, I had to recalibrate my compass. Again, Henri was a compassionate and supportive friend to me during a difficult period of my life, as I hope I was to him.

"What Is Most Important Is Who You Are"

I remember talking about discernment with Henri in 1988, after I had completed my doctorate at Harvard and was practicing as a psychotherapist. By then, some of my spiritual struggles had been resolved. Shaped by Henri's insight, wisdom, and friendship over the past five years, I had decided to reaffirm my Christian identity, even as I continued to attend Buddhist retreats. But I was unsure and conflicted about the next step in my career. Should I work in organizations or keep meeting people as a therapist one-on-one? Should I complete the state requirements to become a licensed clinical psychologist or pursue ordination in the Episcopal Church? Henri's response surprised and worried me. I can't remember the exact details of our conversation, but it went something like this:

Henri said, "I think it's too soon for you to choose any of these."

"Too soon?" I asked, incredulous. "I'm forty years old!" I could feel the familiar tug of critical voices inside me: I'll never be good enough. Henri doesn't respect me. I'm a Christian and a therapist and I still don't know myself. Something's wrong with me.

"You've come a long way in your life," Henri replied, "and there's nothing wrong. It's a journey. You're smart and you have a real gift to offer, but you're focused on a career, and that's not the issue right now. The real question is: What is the ultimate goal of your life? You have one foot in the secular world as a therapist, and you have always had a deep and dynamic spiritual life. It seems as if you see yourself neither in a totally secular professional job nor in a particular religious role. So I don't think this will be easy. You may need to invent a role for yourself, and it will only emerge from a disciplined process of discernment.

"What is most important is who you are. You have to slow down and ask yourself what you really want and what will make you happy and help others to be happy. You need to pray about this. If we follow Jesus and trust Jesus, then we need to adjust our goals in the direction of downward mobility, not upward mobility."

Downward mobility? Hadn't I done enough of that already? I trusted Henri as a friend and mentor, but I resisted his advice. I had grown up in a Lutheran working-class family in northern Wisconsin, and I had worked hard, without my parents' financial help, to get an Ivy League education. After my undergraduate years at Dartmouth, I had lived in a War Resisters League commune in Berkeley and as a back-to-the-lander in rural Vermont, barely supporting myself with odd jobs. As a VISTA volunteer I had worked as a community organizer in the inner city of Kansas City, Missouri. I had taught in a public high school and, for my clinical internship at Harvard, had worked as a psychologist at a school for handicapped people.

Ambition had pushed me into the Ivy League, but I was also drawn to a life of service. How could I integrate my upwardly mobile professional work with being downwardly mobile? I felt America's cultural pull toward individual ambition, accomplishment, and public success. Many of my friends who had envisioned a new, more sustainable way of life had grown tired of being poor and gone on to respectable careers in education, finance, organizational development, and business. I was concerned for the long-term well-being of my family, and I was beginning to wonder: What's wrong with upward mobility, if you're a good person? Maybe it was time for me to make my mark: to go for it—now or never! Yet how did my personal ambition relate to my desire to surrender to God and my longing to serve? I was full of self-doubt and saw no way forward.

Henri said, "Look. What you do follows from who you are. And who you are is the beloved of God. You need to listen to the inner voice of love. There is guidance in that voice. Like all of us, you get stuck when you listen to other voices, especially the self-doubting ones. If you trust in your deep identity as the beloved of God, then your decision will become clear. You'll be more detached from what others say you should want. What you become won't be what you expect or what the American culture expects."

This was an answer without an answer! But over the next few years I came to understand the wisdom of Henri's words. The questions he was asking circulated within me. *Beneath all my doing, who am I being? Who am I? To whom do I belong? Who are my people, and what is my community? What is my deepest desire for my life and for the lives of those I love? What inner voices am I listening to? What brings me joy?*

At some deep level, these questions met others that were emerging from my Buddhist practice. On Buddhist retreats, the Zen master counseled us to investigate simple questions, such as "Who is this who is breathing?" by silently breathing them. As thoughts, worries, memories, and feelings coursed through us, we were encouraged to ask silently, "What is this?" What is this recurring memory, this fear, this longing, or this self-judgment? Such questions challenged us to move past the buzzing confusion of our thoughts, memories, and desires into a silent, intuitive awareness. This kind of self-knowing in solitude seemed to resonate with Henri's advice to slow down and look deeply and carefully into my life. His suggestion that I "befriend" my fears, worries, and aversions was something that I could do anywhere, anytime, including on a Zen retreat.

When I described my dual practice of prayer as a Zen Christian, Henri understood and supported me. He trusted my sense that somehow in the radical emptying of Zen practice, Christ was there, not as an object of my awareness and not as an actual inner voice, but rather as a deep pervasive sense of presence. I was reminded of some of Saint Paul's evocative statements: "It is no longer I who live, but it is Christ who lives in me" (Gal. 2:20

NRSV), "Not I but the grace of God that is with me" (1 Cor. 15:10 NRSV), and "Let the same mind be in you that was in Christ Jesus" (Phil. 2:5 NRSV). Henri invited me to believe that Jesus was not just the historical Jesus of Nazareth, but also the eternal presence of Christ that abides within each person. Christ is somehow within my everyday "I" and within the actual moment-to-moment flow of my thoughts, feelings, memories, and sensations.

My rational mind could not comprehend this, but I felt that it was true; the only way to discover that deep presence directly was in the practice of silent prayer and solitude. Henri called solitude "the furnace of transformation," that dark place in the soul where we shed all distractions and simply wait in trust and faith for the one who calls us the beloved.

One day on a silent Zen retreat at Zen Mountain Monastery in New York, I received a glimpse of what Henri and Saint Paul were talking about. On the third day, after a good deal of angst and hopelessness, the floodgates of my heart broke open, and as tears fell on my meditation cushion I had the distinct feeling that Christ was sitting on the cushion beside me. The thought occurred to me, "Jesus is not afraid of Buddhism. Jesus is not afraid. Jesus is the Incarnation of God, who shares our humanity and wants to know everything about living a finite life. He is the very embodiment of curiosity and creativity. He is within me, and among us, seeks to love everything about me and everything about each person here, and like my Zen master, wants us to reflect deeply and without judgment on the question, what is this?"

I could sense Henri's presence. I recalled his conviction that I could trust myself. My tears fell like rain, a gentle rain of grace.

With Henri's encouragement, I entered Weston Jesuit School of Theology in 1988. Even though I was increasingly estranged from the Vatican, I valued the Roman Catholic understanding of the Eucharist and the Church's mystical heritage. Through my studies at Weston, I sought to rescue the best from the sink-ing boat of my life as a Roman Catholic. Trained at Harvard in object relations psychotherapy, an approach to healing founded on the viewpoint that individual selves are formed through intimate relationships, I wrote my master's thesis at Weston on the intersection of object relations psychotherapy, Christian contemplative prayer, and Buddhist meditation as a path to healing.

Henri was one of my guides, and his voice was one of my own inner voices, but I was gradually putting together my own theology and discovering my own spiritual path.

I joined the Society for Buddhist-Christian Studies, attended some of its national meetings, and became a leader of contemplative practice at its academic gatherings. Then, in the winter of 1994, with Henri's blessing, I opened the Empty Bell, a retreat space located in a renovated carriage house beside our family's new home in Watertown, a suburb of Boston. I founded the Empty Bell as a sanctuary for Buddhist-Christian dialogue and the practice of contemplative prayer, and it became the center of my ministry.

From time to time Henri stayed at our home and came to the Empty Bell to offer Mass. He also attended several interfaith dialogues that I sponsored at the Empty Bell, which gathered together Buddhist and Christian laypeople, monks, and nuns.

During the ten years (1986–96) that Henri lived and worked at Daybreak, we visited each other in person and by phone quite often. After I learned to play the Japanese bamboo flute (shakuhachi), Henri sometimes invited me along when he led retreats. He would get people fired up emotionally about our belovedness in Christ, and then I would stand up and play a contemplative Zen piece, calling attention to the silence between the notes and suggesting that God is present in the silence between our thoughts. Henri often added a masterful teaching about the value of silence and solitude, though I knew that he was often anxious when alone.

Henri was not as interested in Buddhism as I was, but he was intrigued and supportive of my quest; he assured me that the contemplative practices of East and West could enrich each other. When Henri talked about the mind being "a tree full of monkeys," a well-known Buddhist saying, I knew that he was bowing to the East. His ministry was entirely centered on the gospel, whereas mine tacked between Zen and Christianity. This difference between us helped me to keep my own perspective rather than giving myself over completely to Henri's vision. Acknowledging and accepting the ways in which I was differentiating from the Catholic Church and from Henri's distinctive spiritual path reminded me of John Bullitt handing me the wheel on the high seas after a brief period of midshipman training: now you're on your own, but you can trust that the mentor's presence has become a dimension of your own self-awareness.

In the autumn of 1995, Henri spent three months of his sabbatical year living in our home in Watertown. Eight months after his departure, I received a phone call from Henri's secretary, who told me of his death from a heart attack in his homeland of Holland during a stopover on his way to Russia. Deeply grieving, I played the shakuhachi at his funeral in an Orthodox Cathedral near Toronto and at his memorial service in New York City.

Several years later, I joined the board of the Henri Nouwen Society and met Michael Christensen and Rebecca Laird, as well as many other friends of Henri's from different periods of his life. Eventually I compiled two anthologies of his writings, which were published by Orbis and Shambhala Publications.

Over the course of our sixteen years of friendship, Henri and I confided in each other and grew in faith together. We influenced each other, loved each other, disagreed sometimes and had fallings-out, discussed everything from theology and mystical prayer to the benefits of joining a health club, and together fashioned a unique relationship that I never could have anticipated when I first met him. In this we were true to Henri's conviction that discernment is not only a private matter forged in solitude, but also a living flame that needs to be tended in relationship and in community.

Today I continue to lead retreats that focus on Henri's life and teachings. He remains a living presence in my life. I still savor his friendship and benefit from our mutual discernment. Thank you, friend.

Primary Sources and Notations

Introduction: When There Is Darkness, Light

Adapted from the prologue to Nouwen's "Take, Bless, Break, Give," part 1 (unpublished manuscript, 1991); supplemented with an excerpt from *With Open Hands* (Ave Maria Press, 2006), p. 142.

Chapter 1: Embracing the Practice in Solitude and Community

Consolidated and adapted from "Becoming Poor Before God: Spiritual Formation at Daybreak" (unpublished manuscript, 1989); handwritten notes from "God's Will, Acceptance of," (unpublished manuscript, 1990); unpublished excerpts from "The Genesee Diary," (1974), June 11, 29; excerpts from "Power, Powerlessness, and Power: A Theology of Weakness" (August

17, 1993), pp. 1–2; "Prayer as Listening," lecture delivered at "A Conference on Prayer," Woodland Park Community of Celebration, June 23, 1980; and *Gracias!: A Latin American Journal* (Harper & Row, 1983), pp. xviii, 12–13.

Chapter 2: Distinguishing Spirits of Truth and Falsehood

Unpublished excerpts from "The Genesee Diary," "The Road to Daybreak" (working title "The L'Arche Journal"), September 23, November 21, 1985; April 14, 15, May 5, 1986; "South American Diary," November 18, December 14, 1981; unpublished prologue to "Take, Bless, Break, Give" manuscript; and published excerpts from *Bread for the Journey* (HarperSanFrancisco, 2006), November 10, 11, April 15, 1985; *Life of the Beloved* (Crossroad, 2002), pp. 27–28; "Distinguishing Law of the Flesh and Law of the Spirit," in *Gracias!*, p. 13.

Chapter 3: Read the Way Forward

The core content of this chapter is adapted and recontextualized from *Thomas Merton: Contemplative Critic* (Liguori, 1991), especially chapter 2; unpublished excerpts from "L'Arche Diary" and "The Genesee Diary"; lecture notes from "An Introduction to the Spiritual Life" (Yale Divinity School, 1981); Nouwen's introduction to *Desert Wisdom: Sayings from the Desert Fathers,* ed. Yushi Nomura (Doubleday, 1982), p. xii; *Bread for the Journey,* April 15; and *Gracias!,* November 30, 1981.

Chapter 4: Read the Book of Nature

Adapted and integrated from "The Genesee Diary," June 11; *Walk with Jesus: Stations of the Cross* (Orbis, 1990), pp. 3–4; "The Road to Daybreak," January 8, 1986; *Thomas Merton: Contemplative Critic* (Liguori, 1991), pp. 23–24; *Creative Ministry* (Doubleday, 1991), pp. 103–4; *Clowning in Rome* (Image, 2000), pp. 91–93, *Bread for the Journey,* December 9, 10; and *Spiritual Formation* (HarperOne, 2010), pp. 6–7.

Chapter 5: Pay Attention to People in Your Path

Adapted from "L'Arche Journal," August 13, 15, September 9, 10, 23, October 21, November 8, 13, December 21, 1985; *Gracias!*, p. x; November 30, 1981; "Finding Vocation in Downward Mobility," *Leadership* 11, no. 3 (summer 1990): pp. 160–61; *Spiritual Direction* (HarperSanFrancisco, 2006), pp. 5, 116, 123; *Home Tonight* (Image, 2009), p. 107; *Thomas Merton: Contemplative Critic*, (Liguori, 1991), p. 25; and *The Return of the Prodigal Son* (Doubleday, 1992), pp. 21–22.

Chapter 6: Discern the Signs of the Times

Unpublished excerpts from "God's Timeless Time," "L'Arche Journal," June 8, 1986; October 6, 7, 9, 1986. Adapted content from *Thomas Merton: Contemplative Critic*, (Liguori, 1991), pp. 34, 36, 37, 39; *Clowning in Rome*, pp. 130–31; *Bread for the Journey*, September 9, December 6; and *Turn My Mourning into Dancing*, ed. Timothy Jones (Thomas Nelson, 2004), pp. 56, 59.

Chapter 7: Test the Call: Discerning Vocation

Excerpts from "The Genesee Diary," September 1, October 1; "L'Arche Journal," August 4, 1986; "Ukrainian Diary" (unpublished manuscript), July 29; "Sabbatical Journey" (unpublished manuscript); "Finding Vocation in Downward Mobility," pp. 160–61; *Gracias!*, pp. x–xi, xviii, 1, 3, 9, 14; July 29, October 30, 1981; January 20, February 25, 1982.

Chapter 8: Open Your Heart: Discerning Divine Presence

Excerpts from "The Genesee Diary," June 11, September 7, 8, 13, 14, 21, 30, October 1; "South American Diary (Gracias!)," December 2, 1981; "L'Arche Journal," April 2, 13, 1986; "Ukrainian Diary"; "Sabbatical Journey"; "Meditation on Luke 24 Given During the Celebration of Life and Death of Gus van der Woude," April 20, 1975; homily on Luke 24 in class lecture notes (Yale Divinity School, 1981); *With Burning Hearts* (Orbis,

2003), pp. 51, 52, 67, 80, 89, 90; *A Cry for Mercy* (Image, 2002), pp. 125–26, *Gracias!*, December 11, 1981.

Chapter 9: Remember Who You Are: Discerning Identity

Excerpts from "The Life of Faith" (unpublished manuscript, 1988); "The Genesee Diary," August 4; "Ukrainian Diary," August 7, 1993; prologue and introduction from part 1 of "Take, Bless, Break, Give"; *Gracias!*, p. 13; "Being the Beloved," in *Henri Nouwen: Writings,* ed. Robert Jonas (Orbis, 1998), pp. 24–25.

Chapter 10: Know the Time: When to Act, When to Wait, When to Be Led

"A Time to Act" is adapted primarily from Nouwen's sermon preached at Saint Paul's Church, Columbia University, New York City, December 10, 1978; published in *The Road to Peace,* ed. John Dear (Orbis, 1998), pp. 50–52, 110, 124, 198–99.

"A Time to Wait" is adapted primarily from Nouwen's reflections on the spirituality of waiting in lecture notes titled "Waiting" from his course "An Introduction to the Spiritual Life" (Yale Divinity School, 1980); "Power, Powerlessness, and Power"; published in *Finding My Way Home* (Crossroad, 2001), pp. 108–11, 114.

"A Time to Be Led" is adapted primarily from lecture notes entitled "Passion" and "Suffering and New Life" from his course "An Introduction to the Spiritual Life" (Yale Divinity School, 1980); and supplemented by excerpts from *Finding My Way Home,* pp. 91, 95, 96.

Thomas Merton: Contemplative Critic, (Liguori, 1991), pp. 68ff.; *In the Name of Jesus* (Crossroad, 1992), pp. 10, 55, 62, 68–72; *The Road to Peace,* pp. 50–52; *Bread for the Journey,* November 20, 21, April 14; *Gracias!*, March 28; "L'Arche Journal," February 27, 1996.

Epilogue: Discerning the Hidden Wholeness

Condensed and adapted from "One in Christ: Notes on Christian Unity," 1988, file 117, box 34, 1.1 manuscripts, unpublished; "Henri Nouwen: A Conversation Between Friends," interview by Arthur Boers in *The Other Side* (September/October 1989).

Appendix A: We Drink from Our Own Wells: Discernment and Liberation

Condensed from the foreword to *We Drink from Our Own Wells,* by Gustavo Gutiérrez (Orbis, 2003); "Ukrainian Diary II," August 19, 21, 1994; *Gracias!,* pp. viii, 13, November 4; and *Making All Things New* (Harper & Row, 1981), pp. 87–88.

Notes

Preface: *What This Book Is About*
1. Handwritten notes in "God's Will, Acceptance of" (1990), an unpublished short manuscript by Henri Nouwen.

Foreword: *Henri's Way of Discernment*
1. Kenneth L. Woodward, "Soulful Matters" *Newsweek*, October 31, 1994; and Oprah.com article in 2000, at www.oprah.com/omagazine/Hillary-Clinton-On-The-Return-Of-The-Prodigal-Son ixzz207mkposo.
2. Robert A. Jonas, ed. *Henri Nouwen: Writings* (Orbis, 1998), p. 28.

Introduction: *When There Is Darkness, Light*
1. Nouwen wrote this text in 1991 during a writing retreat at Saint Martin d'Aout, France, as an open letter to his friends about

friendship, relationships, Marthe Robin, addictions, death, and spiritual darkness. It is edited and published here for the first time.

Chapter 1: Embracing the Practice in Solitude and Community

1. John Climacus, *The Ladder of Divine Ascent* by John Climacus is quoted by Nouwen in his *Genesse Diary* (1974).
2. Henry David Thoreau, *Walden* (Ticknor and Feilds, 1854), Ch 8.
3. Nouwen also had read Robert J. Voigt's book *Thomas Merton: A Different Drummer* (Liguori Publication, 1972).
4. See Nouwen's *Spirituality of Waiting* audiotape, part 2, published as *The Path of Waiting* (Crossroad, 1995).
5. For a concise treatment of Nouwen's threefold spirituality of *solitude, community,* and *ministry,* see Henri Nouwen, *Spirituality of Living* (Upper Room Books, 2011).
6. For more instructions from Nouwen on the practice of meditative prayer, see *Spiritual Formation* (HarperOne, 2010), pp. 25–28.
7. For concrete instructions from Nouwen on the practice of *lectio divina,* see *Spiritual Direction* (HarperSanFrancisco, 2006), pp. 90–94.

Chapter 2: Distinguishing Spirits of Truth and Falsehood

1. Nouwen also had read the Thomas Merton reader, *A Different Drummer,* Robert Voigt, ed. (Ligouri Publications, 1972).
2. See chapter 9 on discerning our true identity.
3. Quoted in unpublished excerpt from "L'Arche Journal," Monday, October 14, 1985, Feast of Teresa of Avila, p. 85.
4. Nouwen devoted many pages in his journal to Marthe Robin, who, he writes, "continues to inspire others today, who remember her in life and death. She is at the source of much spiritual renewal in France today. There is hardly a new Christian community that is not connected with her in some way. How strange that this little invalid woman did more for our world than the great men and women these days who stand up to preach in stadiums or raise their voices on television." "L'Arche Journal," April 14, 1986; April 15, 1986, pp. 492–96.

5. Prayer of Marthe Robin, translated by Henri Nouwen, "L'Arche Journal," April 15, 1986.

Chapter 3: Read the Way Forward

1. Nouwen met Merton only once, in 1967, while on a short retreat at Gethsemane Abbey in Kentucky, where Thomas Merton was a member. The encounter made a profound impact on Nouwen but is only briefly mentioned in Merton's journal (vol. 6), and Merton records the name incorrectly as "Fr. Nau." Merton died in 1968, and Nouwen began to publish in 1969. Nouwen wrote a book on Merton in Dutch (*Bidden om het leven*) in 1971, while teaching in Amsterdam, which was published the following year in English as *Pray to Live* (Fides, 1972). The book was republished as *Encounters with Merton* (Crossroads, 2004), and informs this chapter.

2. Jean-Pierre de Caussade, *The Sacrament of the Present Moment* (HarperSanFrancisco, 1989), bk. 1, chap. 2, sec. 3.

3. For more reflection by Nouwen on Brother Lawrence's example of daily prayer, see *Spiritual Formation*, p. 24.

4. Thomas Merton, *The Seven Storey Mountain* (Harcourt Brace, 1948).

5. Aseity is the power to exist absolutely in virtue of itself; the reality of God as the essence of existence, or the "pure act of existing" in classical Christian philosophy. The traditional Roman Catholic doctrine that essence and existence are the same in God is grounded in Exodus 3:14, when God declares his true name to Moses: I AM WHO I AM. Patristic writers and scholastic theologians agree that Exodus 3:14 records God declaring himself as pure and simple being. The metaphysical essence of God is existence.

6. Merton, *The Seven Storey Mountain*, p. 172.

7. *The Way of Chuang Tzu, Zen and the Birds of Appetite,* and *Mystics and Zen Masters* are three of Merton's explorations into the wisdom of the East.

8. Merton, *The Seven Storey Mountain*, p. 185.

9. Yushi Nomura, ed., *Desert Wisdom: Sayings from the Desert Fathers* (Doubleday, 1982), p. 4.

10. Merton, *The Seven Storey Mountain*, p. 354.
11. Merton, *The Seven Storey Mountain*, pp. 268–69.
12. Nouwen taught a unit on the discipline of spiritual reading in "An Introduction to the Spiritual Life," Yale Divinity School, 1981.
13. Aelred Squire, ed., *Asking the Fathers* (Paulist Press, 1976), p. 121, quoted in Nouwen's appendix on spiritual reading, "An Introduction to the Spiritual Life" (Yale Divinity School, 1981).
14. Saint Bernard in Advent, sermon 5, quoted in Squire, ed., *Asking the Fathers*, p. 127; quoted in "An Introduction to the Spiritual Life," (Yale Divinity School, 1981).
15. De Caussade, *Letters*, vol. 3, p. 10, quoted in Squire, ed., *Asking the Fathers*, p. 125; quoted in "An Introduction to the Spiritual Life."

Chapter 4: Read the Book of Nature

1. Nouwen might say now that it is easy to think of books as typed pages glued into durable covers or as digital text that can be downloaded electronically into a portable device. But the ancients, like Augustine and others, spoke often of the Book of Nature as worthy of our study. Nouwen agreed with premodern readers that God's first language was nature and wrote about God's messages in nature.
2. Merton, *The Seven Storey Mountain*, p. 293.
3. Theodore Roszak, *The Making of a Counter Culture* (Anchor Books, 1969), p. 245, quoted in Nouwen, *Creative Ministry* (Doubleday, 1991), p. 104.
4. *A Cry for Mercy: Prayers from the Genesee* (Doubleday, 1981), p. 94.

Chapter 5: Pay Attention to People in Your Path

1. Merton, *The Seven Storey Mountain*, p. 219.
2. Merton, *The Seven Storey Mountain*, pp. 195–96.
3. Merton, *The Seven Storey Mountain*, p. 181.
4. In *Wounded Prophet*, Michael Ford provides a catalog of at least 1,500 of Henri's "closest friends." Space and purpose did not allow the editors to include more than three in Henri's most intimate circle, but many other friends could have been included in this section.

5. Nouwen's experience of spending several months in a therapeutic center and his recovery from depression and loss are recounted in the epilogue to *The Road to Daybreak, The Inner Voice of Love,* and the first volume of this series, *Spiritual Direction,* pp. 120–23, on which this version is based.

6. Henri Nouwen did not write as much about his close friendship with Sue Mosteller as he did about his friendship with Jean Vanier, Robert Jonas, and Nathan Ball. Sue first welcomed him to Daybreak in 1985–86, faithfully prayed with him in the chapel every morning for the first hour at Daybreak, traveled with him to France, Holland, and Ukraine, and visited him during his recovery period. Greater in significance than Jonas's gift of friendship and Nathan's offer to become a brother was Sue's willingness to speak God's truth to Henri and thus serve as a living sign of discernment.

7. In her introduction to Henri's last book, *Sabbatical Journey,* Sue Mosteller says that Henri Nouwen mentioned over six hundred friends by name in the over seven-hundred-page journal of his final year, noting connections with over a thousand friends and acquaintants. Truly, human signs of God's presence and direction were most important to Henri Nouwen.

Chapter 6: Discern the Signs of the Times

1. Thomas Merton, *The Literary Essays of Thomas Merton,* ed. Brother Patrick Hart (New Directions, 1981), p. 500.

2. Merton, *The Secular Journal of Thomas Merton* (Dell, 1980), p. 172.

3. Merton, *The Secular Journal,* (Dell, 1980), p. 98.

4. Merton, *My Argument with the Gestapo,* (Doubleday, 1969), p. 138.

5. It is interesting to compare the biblical role of the Tribe of Issachar, who "understood the signs of the times and knew the best course for Israel to take" (1 Chron. 12:32) with Merton's conception of discerning the signs of the times.

6. Note Nouwen's eyewitness account of civil rights actions in Selma and his presence at the funeral of Martin Luther King Jr. in Atlanta are recorded in *The Road to Peace.*

7. About the "unmasking of illusion," Merton writes: "The world as pure object is something that is not there. It is not a reality outside

us for which we exist. . . . It is a living and self-creating mystery of which I am myself a part, to which I am myself, my own unique door. When I find the world in my own ground, it is impossible for me to be alienated by it." *Contemplation in a World of Action* (University of Notre Dame Press, 1999), pp. 154–55.

8. *Seeds of Contemplation* (Farrar, Straus and Giroux, 1990), p. 53.

Chapter 7: Test the Call: Discerning Vocation

1. Nouwen's "South American Journal" from October 1981 to March 1982 was published as *Gracias!* (HarperCollins, 1982).

Chapter 8: Open Your Heart: Discerning Divine Presence

1. Quoted in "The Genesee Diary," September 23.
2. Anthony Bloom, *Beginning to Pray* (Paulist Press, 1970), p. 75.
3. See chapters 1 and 3 on the practice of *lectio divina*.
4. Philosophically, *Dasein* is one of the core terms in Heidegger's *Being and Time*, referring to an entity that is conscious of the meaning of its own existence or presence. John Eudes, referring to Heidegger's philosophy of being, applies the term to the Roman Catholic understanding of the "real presence" of Christ in the Eucharist under the "appearance" of bread and wine. Appearance is something that announces or reveals itself without showing itself fully. For more on the concept of *Dasein*, see Martin Heidegger, *Being and Time*, trans. by Joan Stambaugh (Albany: State University of New York Press, 1996).
5. Nouwen's unpublished summary of John Eudes's reflection on the Eucharist at the Feast of Corpus Christi in the Abbey of the Genesee, edited and adapted from Nouwen's journal, vol. 1, June 11, 1974, pp. 41–43.
6. In the spirituality of Evagrius Ponticus, Dorothee of Gaza, Diadoque, John Climacus, Cassien, and Saint Benedict, we find this philosophical insight emphasized. For them, the divine presence is revealed in the heart in prayer, meditation, and *ascesis* (Gr. from *askein*, "to exercise")—the spiritual exercise of self-discipline in pursuit of contemplative ideals for religious purpose. Nouwen's re-

search notes in "The Genesee Diary," September 21 and October 12, 1973.

7. In the spirituality of Saint John Chrysostom, Theodore of Mopsuestia, and later in Bernard of Clairvaux, this concept of memory prevails, according to Nils A. Dahl. In Aristotle's psychological theory of memory, *to remember* (*mnemoneuein*) is properly applicable only to events of the past, whereas in the New Testament it may also refer to present or future occurrences. Thus, in addition to signifying "to recollect," it can also mean to think of someone or something (Col. 4:18), or to mention in prayer (Rom. 1:9; 1 Thess. 1:2; Eph. 1:16). According to Dahl, "This enlargement of the Greek concept in the New Testament reflects the influences of the Jewish cultus and tradition. In the Old Testament, God remembers His People and they in turn are called upon to remember God's mighty acts of salvation and His commandments." Dahl's examination of the literature leads him to conclude that memory and commemoration occupied a central place in the worship, preaching to the churches, and prayer and thanksgiving of early Christianity. From Nouwen's research notes and summary of Yale professor Nils A. Dahl's essay, "Anamnesis: Memory and Commemoration in Early Christianity," originally published in French in *Studia Theological I* (1947), pp. 69–95.

Chapter 9: Remember Who You Are: Discerning Identity

1. *Theosis,* or deification (literally "becoming God"), is the ancient theological concept used to describe the process by which Christians become more like God until they are fully divine. For an extensive history of this Christian doctrine, see Michael J. Christensen and Jeffery Wittung, eds., *Partakers of the Divine Nature: The History and Development of Deification in the Christian Traditions* (Baker Academic, 2008).

2. For Nouwen's full teaching on "Claiming our Belovedness," see *Life of the Beloved* (Crossroad, 2002); and *Spiritual Direction,* chap. 10.

Chapter 10: know the time: When to Act, When to Wait, When to Be Led

1. *Conjectures of a Guilty Bystander* (Image, 1968), p. 156.

2. Praying at the stations of the cross is a devotional practice in the Roman Catholic Church to commemorate the fourteen events between Jesus's being condemned to death by Pontius Pilate and his burial in a borrowed tomb, often vividly portrayed in paintings and sculptures throughout the common era.

3. The early 1980s in the United States was a time of cultural fear and increasing risk of nuclear war. As the nuclear freeze movement gained momentum, Nouwen became more concerned and socially active in denouncing U.S. militarism, nuclear arsenals, and war. He wrote a book about the spirituality of peacemaking and publicly protested nuclear arms testing in Nevada and U.S. intervention in Latin American countries. However, as a Dutch citizen living in the United States, he never felt called to let himself be arrested and go to jail for the sake of peace. "I have always wondered if my going to jail would not alienate people from the cause of peace rather than attract them to it," he states in his "Peaceworks" manuscript. "But maybe I am concerned too much about influencing others and not enough about faithfulness to my own spiritual commitment." *The Road to Peace,* p. 54.

4. Among the many events in Central America that Nouwen describes in his writings on social action is the rise to power of General Ríos Montt in Guatemala in 1982. He claimed to be an ardent follower of Jesus, and Evangelical and Pentecostal church leaders claimed him as one of their own. Yet, within months of his Christian leadership of the army, at least 2,600 peasants had been killed under his orders (see *The Road to Peace,* p. 13). Nouwen wrote about what he witnessed and the stories he heard in Guatemala in *Love in a Fearful Land: A Guatemalan Story* (Ave Maria Press, 1985).

5. Biographical note: In the summer of 1983, Nouwen visited Nicaragua for a month, and joined a Witnesses for Peace delegation on the border of Honduras. There he witnessed the conflict between the U.S.-supported contras and the Sandinistas, and heard stories

from the mothers about the torture and murder of their children. Upon his return to the United States to teach at Harvard Divinity School, he felt compelled to call on the Christian community in North America to oppose the Reagan administration's invasion of Central America. With the support of several peace groups, he embarked on a six-week national speaking tour to raise awareness of the injustices being committed in the countries where he had visited church leaders and poor people. One of the churches he preached at during his tour was our church—Golden Gate Community Church of the Nazarene in San Francisco—where he shared his call to contemplation and action.

6. Simone Weil, *First and Last Notebooks* (Oxford University Press, 1970).

7. For an extended reflection on vocation and leadership, see *In the Name of Jesus* (Crossroads, 1989), on which this section is based.

Appendix A: We Drink from Our Own Wells: Discernment and Liberation

1. Gustavo Gutiérrez's seminal *A Theology of Liberation* (Orbis, 1972) emerged in Latin America in the late 1960s and was published in Spanish in 1971. The book quickly became a clarion call to a "preferential option for the poor." Gustavo became known as the father of Liberation Theology, a practical theology born out of solidarity with the people. His books and courses became prophetic in the Liberation Theology movement in Latin America and around the world. In the dialectic between Nouwen's more contemplative spirituality and Gustavo's more activist faith, a new kind of liberationist spirituality was articulated that is reflected in Gustavo's *We Drink from Our Own Wells* and Henri's foreword to the book.

2. Although Nouwen remained critical of some aspects of Liberation Theology, what impressed him most was how Gustavo Gutiérrez integrated mysticism and activism, the struggle for spiritual growth and the struggle for political freedom. In his development of a "liberation spirituality," Gutiérrez draws on the primordial waters of spiritual experience: oral tales and written texts, con-

crete lives and communities of faith, in the common struggle for freedom.

3. Upon his return in the spring of 1982, Harvard Divinity School offered him a position as Lentz Lecturer to give public lectures on the spiritual aspects of Liberation Theology. The following fall, he was appointed professor of divinity with the provision that he would teach one semester each year and be free to travel to Latin America and pursue other interests during the other semester. Two years later, he revisited the question of vocation, discerned that it was time to leave academia, and began to seek a spiritual home among those with physical and mental disabilities at L'Arche Community in France. See *The Road to Daybreak,* Nouwen's discernment journal leading from Harvard to L'Arche Daybreak in Toronto.

Appendix B: Henri Nouwen on Hearing a Deeper Beat

1. Summarized from Nouwen's handwritten notes in "God's Will, Acceptance of" (unpublished manuscript, 1990).

2. According to Mickey Hart, drummer for the Grateful Dead: "The drum circle offers equality because there is no head or tail. It includes people of all ages. The main objective is to share rhythm and get in tune with each other and themselves. To form a group consciousness. To resonate. . . . A new voice, a collective voice, emerges from the group as they drum together." Testimony before the U.S. Senate Special Committee on Aging, 1991.

3. Henry David Thoreau (1817–62) was a contrarian thinker, writer, and activist. At a time when others were ecstatic over the prospects of industrial development, he championed the cause of protecting the environment. While others embraced the practice of slavery, he was an outspoken abolitionist. He went to jail for refusing to pay his taxes rather than support a government that wanted to expand slavery into Mexico. He was among the first to advocate nonviolent civil disobedience. Philosophically, he was a transcendentalist and a deist. He believed that the best way to know God was through personal intuition rather than religious doctrine.

4. "Order my steps in Your word. . . . I want to walk worthy, my calling fulfill. Please order my steps, Lord, and I'll do Your blessed will. The world is ever changing, but You are still the same; if You order my steps, I'll praise Your name." "Order My Steps," lyrics by Glen Bruleigh.

5. *Spiritual Formation,* p. xxiii. The four steps of *lectio divina:* read, meditate, pray, rest.

6. C. S. Lewis, *The Silver Chair* (HarperCollins, 2001), p. 560.

7. In the Bible, Gideon "put out the fleece" to discern God's will (Judg. 6:36–40). "Then Gideon said to God, 'If you are truly going to use me to rescue Israel as you promised, prove it to me in this way. I will put a wool fleece on the threshing floor tonight. If the fleece is wet with dew in the morning but the ground is dry, then I will know that you are going to help me rescue Israel as you promised'" (Judg. 6:36–37 NLT).

8. For Methodists, God speaks primarily through scripture, church tradition, and reason. According the Nouwen, God has many ways to get through to us and illuminate our path, so that we don't lose our way.

9. *Thomas Merton: Contemplative Critic,* p. 37.

10. See chapter 6.

Credits

Good faith efforts have been made to credit and obtain permissions for pieces quoted or adapted in this work. If any required acknowledgments have been omitted or any rights overlooked, it is unintentional. Please notify the publishers of any omission, and it will be rectified in future editions.

Grateful acknowledgment is made for permission to adapt previously published work of Henri J. M. Nouwen:

Excerpts from four books published by HarperOne: *Making All Things New* (© 1981); *Gracias! A Latin American Journal* (© 1983); *Bread for the Journey* (© 1997); and *Spiritual Formation* (© 2010).

Excerpts from *Thomas Merton: Contemplative Critic* (Liguori Publications, 1991, by special arrangement with Harper & Row). Originally published as *Pray to Live* (Fides, 1972); republished as *Encounters with Merton* (Crossroad, 2004).

Unpublished portions from original diaries and journals: "On Retreat: Genesee Diary" (3 bound volumes, 1974), June 11, 29, 23, July 3, 6, 20–23, 25, 30; August 4, 8,15, 20, 21; Sept. 18, 21–22, 27, 30; Oct. 14, 18–23; Nov 22; Dec. 2, 8. "South American Diary" (1981–1982): Nov. 19, 1981; Dec. 31, 1981, Jan. 27, 1982, Feb.15, 1982. "The L'Arche Journal" (1985–1986); August 26, 27, Sept. 13, 22, 23, 27; Oct. 5, 8, 14, 21, 22, 23, 25, 30; Nov. 1, 13, 20, 21; Dec. 15, 1985; Jan. 3,7, 8, 13, 21, 28, 29; Feb. 2, 9, 13, 16, 18, 22, 27; March 2, 3, 11, 13, 23, 24; April 2, 3, 13–20, 24, 27; May 1, 30; June 4, 8, 15, 16; July 2, 7, 11; Aug. 4, 5; Sept. 21, 30; Oct. 1, 6, 7, 8, 1986. "Ukrainian Diary" (1993), July 28, 29.

Class lecture notes on "Waiting," "Passion," and "Suffering and New Life." Notes on Nils A. Dahl's essay "Anamnesis: Memory and Commemoration in Early Christianity" in course materials for "An Introduction to the Spiritual Life," Yale Divinity School, 1980.